Love Sick: One Woman's Journey through Sexual Addiction

"*Love Sick* provides an honest and deeply chilling account of
what it's like to suffer from a compulsion to look for love
in what are most definitely all the wrong places."
—Francine Prose, *Elle*

"A self-proclaimed addict looks unflinchingly at the
source of her sickness and her road to recovery."
—*O* (*Oprah Magazine*)

"Compelling. . . . Silverman explores the psychology of addiction
on a deeply personal level. Candid, emotionally raw . . .
never sugarcoated. . . . Deeply moving."
—*Booklist*

"Thanks in large part to fearless writers such as Silverman,
our culture is confronting the wretched behaviors that
exist even in homes with facades of normalcy."
—Mary Ann Lindley, *Tallahassee Democrat*

"In the existing literature on sexual addiction, this book stands
alone: a woman's narrative of her own personal story. As self-help,
Love Sick will resonate with not only those who suffer from sexual
addiction, but also anyone whose compulsive behavior, whether
with drugs, money, or food, threatens his or her emotional well-being.
And as memoir, Silverman's account is an important literary
accomplishment, one that will move anyone who reads it."
—*recoveryworld.com*

"Silverman's stark story of struggle and recovery, told without jargon or
psychobabble, creates a wrenching portrait many women will relate to—
a portrait of someone who is looking for love, but finds sex instead."
—*Lifetime-TV*

"Silverman is a wonderful writer. With her searing honesty, sharp perceptions, and ability to convey the nuances of emotional terrain, she sheds light on a topic that has been shrouded in secrecy and muddled in misperceptions."

—Deborah Tannen, *New York Times* bestselling author

Because I Remember Terror, Father, I Remember You

"Beautiful, rocketing prose."

—*Tallahassee Democrat*

"Silverman's lyric style transforms a ravaged childhood into a work of art. The book reads like a poem."

—*St. Petersburg Times*

"A rough emotional ride, but it is well worth it."

—*Ms. Magazine*

"Profoundly moving in its portrait of a child's fear, confusion, and desperate search for a safe place."

—*Kirkus Reviews*

"Searing, brave, powerfully written. . . . Silverman's memoir is about more than incest: it is about evil, about denial, about the great chasm between the public facade of a prominent, successful family and its painful reality, and it is about how, as in a Greek tragedy, a curse has been passed down through several generations. This book is the cry that shatters that curse."

—Adam Hochschild, author of *King Leopold's Ghost: A Story of Greed, Terror, and Heroism in Colonial Africa*

"A terrifying and heartening book. I know it is going to be passed urgently from hand to hand."

—Rosellen Brown, *New York Times* bestselling author

HOW TO SURVIVE DEATH
AND OTHER INCONVENIENCES

American Lives Series

Tobias Wolff, editor

HOW TO SURVIVE
DEATH
AND OTHER
INCONVENIENCES

SUE WILLIAM SILVERMAN

University of Nebraska Press | Lincoln

Acknowledgments for the use of copyrighted
material appear on page 195, which constitutes
an extension of the copyright page.

Library of Congress Cataloging-in-Publication Data
Names: Silverman, Sue William, author.
Title: How to survive death and other
inconveniences / Sue William Silverman.
Description: Lincoln: University of Nebraska Press,
[2020] | Series: American lives series | Includes
bibliographical references.
Identifiers: LCCN 2019030461
ISBN 9781496214096 (paperback: alk. paper)
ISBN 9781496220998 (epub)
ISBN 9781496221001 (mobi)
ISBN 9781496221018 (pdf)
Subjects: LCSH: Silverman, Sue William. | Fear of
death. | Death—Humor. Classification: LCC BF789.
D4 S545 2020 | DDC 818/.603 [B]—dc23
LC record available at
https://lccn.loc.gov/2019030461

Set in Garamond Premier Pro by Laura Ebbeka.
Designed by L. Auten.

For

Jamie Christie who helped me survive adolescence

Randy Groskind (in memoriam) who helped me survive myself

The Hypnotist who helped me survive my memories

All the women, dearest friends, who help me survive, period

Vermont College of Fine Arts that helps us all
survive through the written word

Marc J. Sheehan, with love, who helps me survive every day

Quizzle, the Magical Cat, who survives in my memory

How is it possible, after all, that someone should simply vanish? How can someone who lived, loved, and wrangled with God and with himself just disappear? I don't know how and in what sense but they're here. Since time is an illusion, why shouldn't everything remain?

—Isaac Bashevis Singer

I am a woman of words. Take away my words and what is left of me?

—Terry Tempest Williams

When death finds you, may it find you alive.

—African proverb

Contents

FATE 2 LACHESIS

measures the thread of life to determine how long you live

FATE 3 ATROPOS

cuts the thread of life with a pair of shears to decide how someone dies

Author's Note

In this book I explore memory as a way of surviving death. Obviously, my memories are mine and mine alone. My recollections—of events, of people, of myself—shift and change over the years as memories tend to do. In short, as I evolve, so do my memories, showing new facets of themselves. As Oliver Sacks says, "We now know that memories are not fixed or frozen . . . but are transformed, disassembled, reassembled, and re-categorized with every act of recollection."

Which is to say that other people who shared these encounters might remember things differently. Everyone brings a unique past to an experience and carries away a unique future.

The past as conveyed in this book takes place in compressed time and in non-chronological order, yet I have endeavored to be accurate in these acts of recollection. Some names and details have been changed to protect people's privacy.

ULTIMA THULE

rimestock: old almanacs with runic writings

For example: "This rimestock contains signs, symbols, and
the secret knowledge of archaic words that refuse to die."

My odyssey to survive death begins like any other ordinary metaphysical road trip.

In 2014, in my house in Michigan, I flip open my 1972 *Hammond's
Contemporary World Atlas* to pinpoint exact locations from my past.
Not just where I lived, but specific events.

I suffer an existential crisis at a wedding reception here.
I relive lost teenage years at an Adam Lambert concert here.
I have sex in an emergency room here.
I survive death here *and* here *and* there.
Tupperware mishap? Right here.
And so on . . .

The atlas is a "new" census edition, including a "Gazetteer-Index of
the World." Never mind that the atlas is woefully out of date. This way
it's easier to envision the past, back, for example, when the population
of the United States is 203,184,772, back when Siam is (Thailand) only
in parentheses, and Persia (Iran). And who knows which countries
in the atlas—tinted green, yellow, blue—exist today, since I never
bought a more recent one. Of course it's difficult to miss the demise
of Yugoslavia, but what about Ascension? Ceylon, French Guiana,

Surinam, Swaziland, Tokelau Islands, White Russia. Some of these countries still exist, some don't, some still breathing, others defunct, as if a country itself can die.

The population of Glen Rock, New Jersey, in 1972, where I attended high school, is 13,010. The state flower is the violet, the state bird the Eastern Goldfinch.

*Gold*finch. The same color as that Plymouth in which I cruised Route 17 for hours, days, or seemingly forever. In fact, metaphorically speaking, I'm *still* behind the wheel even though the Plymouth is, no doubt, a rusted husk by now. And even though I left Jersey years ago, I'm still cruising through life, planning never to stop.

North Jersey, around Route 17 back then, was known for chemical, metal, plastic products, and oil refining.

Were goldfinches able to survive that? Or is the entire species now extinct?

I also open a frayed 1967 AAA map of the State of New Jersey. My gaze follows Route 17, a white thread hemmed by red lines on either side, a divided highway, from Secaucus to Paramus, past Saddle River, to the end of the line.

What happens there? After a jagged snippet of New York, the map terminates with a solid black border. On the other side is the unknowable. White space. Just looking at that blank expanse, I feel afloat on a medieval map, in Ultima Thule, where clawed sea creatures lurk beyond the edges of the known world.

But isn't Death the ultimate Ultima Thule, the final boundary between the known and unknown worlds? What conditions must exist, what to pack in your carry-on, how to prepare to cross that liminal threshold from the State of Being to Non-Being? Better yet: How to escape it altogether? Or is death a great adventure like climbing Mt. Everest that would surely kill me in any event.

What does it feel like to actually die?

Even though I'm convinced I can outsmart, outrun, sidestep, or certainly outdrive and outdistance death in that gold Plymouth, still I spend hours obsessing about it. What is the appearance of the Ultima Thule of Death? Do I find it or does it find me? What does it sound like, taste like? Does death have a voice? Is it pure absence? I might not fear death if I could be alive to experience it.

To study death I ignore words such as "void" and "abyss." I dismiss the words "nothingness," "oblivion." While these default words associated with death *might* be relevant, they're too abstract to convey the tangibility of it.

Is death like floating in a red haze to a distant horizon? Is it experiencing your molecules rearrange themselves, blending into the gray vapor of space? Does your shadow shimmer in a lattice of black-and-white starshine: a vague form only partially visible? Or does your soul shapeshift like phases of the moon? Is death ascending into a Time beyond Time? Or if I don't ascend maybe I descend, entering Earth's depth: the grit of dirt, the dampness of pure weather. Maybe it's becoming merely elemental. Solid, liquid, gaseous, isotopic. Tasting xenon, inhaling palladium, hearing tin and tellurium, seeing the world through carbon-plated eyes. Does my heart turn to krypton? My mind to osmium?

But these items belong to *this* world? So is death (more or less; give or take) simply the loss of ceramic plates, couches, bedspreads, forks, spoons of our everyday existence? I mean, who is going to care for these things, *my* things, after (*if*) I die? I worry about this. Really! I do.

I also worry that my consciousness, *if* death occurs, will evaporate into a sensory isolation chamber, unaware of even following a thin red highway until it evanesces off the map of charted existence into _____. *What?*

Here I must insert a blank space to be filled in after the fact. Which will be difficult to do if "after" doesn't exist. Is either the meaning or the actuality of death the ultimate fill-in-the-blank quiz? And will I fail the test because you can't grip a pencil with skeletal fingers?

Is death the inability to write a full sentence? In death can you write only a fragment? Is death one word searching in vain for a mate? A lost syllable? A misplaced letter? Is death an absence of key words or lost language?

If my body has a breakdown, am I left as only a footnote or erasure? A blank page?

I plan to never find out.

How can I *not* fear death? I don't know where the throb in my heart would beat if it stopped. Who would care for it? Where do veins thrum when blood evaporates? Where do lungs go when they slow to a shudder? A pulse slips out, reverberating dark streets, useless. The crease between my eyebrows—or yours—splits the skull. Breath exhales past my lips—or yours.

My pupils wouldn't know what to see, so they'd see everything and nothing. I would be a hint of air seeping through glass, a palm pressed against a flash of light.

The fear itself, never mind the actual fact, is combustible, desperate. Not believing in a god or a religion, I don't await a heavenly Afterlife. I am on my own.

What follows, then, is an essential and indispensable guide to survive death on my own terms.

The plan contains 3 Easy Steps:

STEP 1: Preserve Memories. I flip through musty pages of the atlas, here in my restored Victorian house in Michigan, to begin this quest on the Highway of Lost Memories, cruising in the gold Plymouth, to discover myself in every place I've visited or lived. These places, these selves, these memories exist because I exist; I exist because they exist.

Once found, hoard memories. They keep you alive.

On the one hand, memory holds the past in place like exhibits behind glass in my personal, internal museum. This desire to grasp the past is at one with my desire to hold onto life. On the other hand, each memory embraces what happens *after* events first take place, thus revealing itself anew, creating a palimpsest: the past affecting the present, and the present reshaping memory.

Therefore, it's what memory makes of an event that matters more than the event itself.

STEP 2: I revive archaic, obsolete, and obscure words just as I hope, when needed, to revive myself. *All* words are necessary, must be at the ready, in order to maintain memories—and a self—forever.

STEP 3: Use these words to examine and explore memory. Construct memory into tangible living-and-breathing sensory images, thus resulting in a life's immortal narrative.

IN SUM: To survive death, mix words and memories together with a pinch of scent, a flask of taste, a kaleidoscope of sound, and allow it all to marinate for eternity.

To survive death you have to believe in magic, language, and memory.

I do.

You have to be metaphoric. Transformative. Nostalgic.

I was. And I am.

I refuse to seize the day. I seize the past and conjure it into an always-alive present, the never-never-ending future.

You have to believe in Van Gogh's endless circle of life: "The earth had been thought to be flat. Science has proven that the earth is round. They persist in believing that life is flat and runs from birth to death. However, life, too, is probably round."

Just as memory is round, always circling. If a memory haunts me, it keeps me alive until I figure it out. I hope never to fully figure it out. Memory: its own life-form.

Through memory, I must also discover why—if death terrifies me—I taunt it.

Death: Catch me if you can!

FATE 1 CLOTHO

spins the thread of life

THE ETERNAL REIGN
OF MISS ROUTE 17

agerasia: quality of not growing old

For example: "This road trip of my life is specifically
designed to achieve agerasia: to outrun, outdistance, outlast
The Three Fates who stalk my every move."

I floor the accelerator of my parents' gold Plymouth Savoy. I abandon
the immaculate green lawns of Glen Rock, New Jersey, looking for
action. Soft vowelly suburban teenage boys—Joey, Bruce, Howie—
diminish in the rearview. As does a future that would also be dimin-
ished by starched shirtwaist dresses, primly flipped hair, Ivory-soaped
skin. I seek other names and places to discover and define who I am
and what I want: more or less to live forever.

In high school my definition of "life," of "action," of "forever" is
modest—to hurtle up and down Route 17—blaring the Supremes,
the Rolling Stones, the Beatles. Here, I'm free, electric, invincible. To
survive death I *must* be invincible, just like Route 17, where acidic rain
and lightning illuminate "Eat Here" signs atop diners. The limitless
wet sky thunders my car to the pavement. Route 17 shivers intensely,
embracing me in its rumbling sounds. At dusk, when the rain stops, I
roll down the window and inhale a bouquet of diesel fumes. Coppery
strobes of sunset reflect off car bumpers. Where else do I want to be?
Nowhere, is where.

When streetlights and neon ignite, I, underage, sneak into bars
and play foosball and pinball. I plunk spare change into the jukebox. I

dance with anyone who asks—Rick, Steve—guys skulking hard-edged consonants. Camel cigarettes are tucked in the sleeves of their white T-shirts like small packets of death. But we're safe here with all the power of Route 17 keeping us alive.

Or these guys and I hang out in parking lots. We barely speak, mesmerized by Ford Galaxies, Chevy Bel Airs, Plymouth Furies finning down the highway. I love the bars, the boys, the parking lots, the smell of asphalt, smoke, sulphur. Soot smudges the sky like charcoal kisses that last longer than dime-store Raspberry Heaven lipstick. I lean against my car, heat from the engine rising up my spine like warm toxic sap.

Soon I'm back behind the wheel steering toward midnight. I pass Esso and Sinclair stations, drive-in movie theaters, bowling alleys, stores selling Rheingold and Bud. Wind from trucks scours the pavement. Clanking trains blast down the tracks. Creosote from factory chimneys trails after me, clotting my lungs with indestructible chemicals, Route 17 seeping into me with its industrial lust.

Some weekends, however, I stay home in my quiet suburb. I awake as if hungover: too much Route 17 to absorb on any given night.

Glen Rock days I sit on the spotless curb in front of my house, summer slanting over rooftops of identical brick ranch homes. How can you not love the perfection of such order: wall-to-wall carpets; rectangular windows unsmudged by exhaust, the always sunny days reflecting off glass; spotless stainless-steel kitchens. All the stop signs freshly painted red.

I pluck clover and weave stems into delicate chains. At the swimming pool, I'm groggy with chlorine, a mist of summer I want to believe will last into infinity. I suck Kool-Aid ice cubes until my tongue is the color of cherries or blood.

So isn't the suburb too stifling, too perfect, too deadly to be in the running for "Best Place Never to Die, Ever"?

The suburbs are like mercury enclosed in glass: always measuring a too-cool, nondescript, barely alive temperature. Route 17, on the other hand, is splintered glass, quicksilver spilling across a feverish, macadam night: enough artificiality to survive nuclear attacks, plagues, an "F" in home economics.

Which location is my best bet to keep me alive forever? I put my money on Route 17.

I particularly need Route 17 now, about to leave Jersey for college. Again, again, the Plymouth and I are tugged to its asphalt force field. The bottoms of my thighs, in pedal pushers, sweat against white vinyl. Sun burns my left forearm pressed to the chrome window ledge. The car smacking into potholes keeps me awake. It all does: the heat, the sweat, the jolting, the metal. I love that the Plymouth is a Savoy. I am the sole occupant of a mobile hotel swinging through the bass beat of Jersey.

When I reach Deadman's Circle, I hit the gas. I spin around the circle once, twice, as if driving an amusement park bumper car, daring death to catch me in this never-ending cycle. I swerve to avoid an unamused driver inching into the roundabout from a side street. He honks. I wave, smile, and press on, driving faster.

Although deathless itself, Route 17 assists in murdering the northern New Jersey wetlands. The Meadowlands is a lab test. The refuse in landfills steams all day, all night. Pesticides simmer in a slow flame. Iridescent rainbows oil the irradiated surface of evaporating puddles, leaving behind a suicide note written in neon and perfidy.

My father, a banker, funds loans for such development. Visiting his bank located off Route 17, I enter air scented with money. A few years later my father also becomes a member of the Meadowlands Commission that helps develop Giants Stadium.

Route 17 will never die. Development will never die. Nor will the memory of all this nonbiodegradable beauty.

Do I recognize that then or only now? How does memory preserve itself? Is it like a postcard of a scenic overlook on personal history? *Wish you were here!* Yes. But memory *also* preserves itself by rippling through time, reinventing itself: a new postcard with a different sentiment every year. Memory is magic: both static and fluid.

What, I now wonder, remains of that gold, sadly mortal Plymouth? Surely in some landfill outside Passaic one ingot of this car still exists shining from beneath mounds of refuse. Route 17 at least will always continue even though, unlike Route 66, it will never have a hit TV show or a popular song. It only has me—Miss Route 17—to sing its praises.

After a local newspaper advocates for the elimination of Deadman's Circle, it is replaced by a conventional intersection controlled by traffic lights. A thirty-mile-long barrier replaces the grass median in the 1970s, the same decade the highway north of Paramus becomes eight lanes. In the 1980s, an overpass condemns the last traffic light.

But that hasn't happened yet. And Route 17 still thrives, anyway.

I swerve, without signaling, into the parking lot of a diner, curved and silvery as an Airstream trailer. I slam on the brakes. Almost dusk, dyed-to-perfection rose-gold sunlight reflects off the metallic surface. A boy and girl kiss in a car parked a few spaces down from me. He wears Army fatigues, and I know, or imagine to know, he's shipping off for Vietnam in the morning. Their windows are closed, the air-conditioning running.

I sit in my car waiting. For something. For the moment when the essence of Route 17 will rise up around me, when I become one with the highway, embody it. I rest my head on the seat back and close my eyes. Horns, air brakes, tires. A siren in the distance—sounds of emergencies—reminding me I am the one still breathing.

I cross the parking lot and push open the door to the diner. The sudden blast of cold feels like brain freeze behind my eyes. I order a burger, fries, chocolate milk shake, food with enough preservatives to transmogrify my iffy human cells into an immortal New Jersey goddess.

After eating I hit the road. A mile down the highway, the neon sign on the bowling alley outlines a ball rocketing into pins over and over. It beckons. Inside, I slip into rented shoes, scuffed and worn, smelling of sweat. How could I be happier, what with my hair teased and sprayed to an impermeable Aqua Net helmet? Eyelids shadowed. Lips opalescent pink. Red-and-blue neon beer signs flash. The jukebox rocks. It rolls. The lanes swirl with solider-than-solid bowling balls. Pins clatter. The setup racks rattle into place. I love all the clanking, the thudding, the huzzahs. After securing a lane, I slip fingers and thumb into the holes of a turquoise ball. I hug it to my chest. I step onto the polished wood floor. I fling the iridescent ball down the alley. It wavers and wobbles to the end knocking down three pins. My next ball gutters. Who cares? There's always another rapturous swirl down the alley.

A guy at the intersection of juvenile delinquency and ruin slouches over offering beer and a jaundiced smile. I smile back. My crush on him is immediate and hard. I see him the next night and the next in the bowling alley. During the day waiting for him, lost in the mirage of heat shimmering off asphalt, *I* feel jaundiced, my throat parched with dengue-like fever, teenage drama to the nth degree, energizing me.

The crush lasts all summer. Until fall. When the fever finally breaks to a fine blue stubble of desire. Only then do I realize it's a lesser crush than my one on Route 17. Or maybe he was only metonymous with Route 17. He's part of my fever—a form of limerence, acute longing, haunting thoughts and desires—to possess all the gaudy, everlasting artificial life it offers. Route 17, all lit up like Vegas, is better, because it's real.

After saying 'bye to the boy in the bowling alley, I, once again behind the wheel, reenter the stream of headlights and taillights. No actual stars are visible—which eventually burn out anyway—only neon. I vibrate in all the flowing, blinking, streaming, twinkling as the Jersey night smears past.

Hemingway said all true stories end in death. But he wasn't from Jersey, so what did he know? Or maybe Jon Bon Jovi was right when he said heaven looks a lot like New Jersey. Regardless, in this moment, whether

Heaven or Hell, the Plymouth is my current means of transportation for surviving it, outdistancing it.

Who knows what's possible when you undertake a road trip mapped to discover a route with bridges and tunnels, detours and alternate byways, to circumvent death—driving through Time not just Space—steering among past, present, future peregrinations without end.

Don't live or think or remember or drive as the crow flies. Live like your memories, which exist in loops and mazes and circles within traffic circles.

Surviving death is labyrinthine. Every stop along the way, every scenic overlook, is part of the story of survival: every word—resurrected archaic or current slang—every discovered memory, every off-and-on-ramp, every exit and turnoff. Every entrance. Nothing is insignificant.

I pull my glittering Plymouth time machine to the side of the road near an outdoor movie screen. The engine idles. Giant movie stars, night after night, hover godlike over the awed assembly: Paul Newman, Elizabeth Taylor, Warren Beatty, Natalie Wood. Their starry faces glow, projected against the backdrop of night. The movies end. Cars roll from the lot. Tinny voices, through speakers knocked from their posts and dangling on frayed wires, call out: *Come back, my darling.*

Call out: *My God, it's alive!*

13 WAYS OF SURVIVING
NEW JERSEY

venustation: act of causing to become beautiful

anvenustation (antonym): act of causing to become unbeautiful

1.

On July 11, the anniversary of the duel between Aaron Burr and Alexander Hamilton, I swerve off Route 17 and drive the gold Plymouth to the Palisades. I sit on a rock beside the historical marker noting Hamilton's demise though, officially, he died in New York City the next day. I want to ask Hamilton: Was it worth it? The answer must be *no*, though at least his marker offers a stupendous view overlooking the Hudson River and the Manhattan skyline. Not bad for a loser. Not a bad location to be struck the final blow. Generations will visit you, or this spot, keeping you, albeit not the corporeal you, alive.

2.

I remain seated on the rock beside the Hamilton marker. The warmth still seems to contain the heat of the duel, the flash of a movie camera. The Palisades also hosted the filming of many early silent-movie pictures. The first studios were in New York, and filmmakers crossed the Hudson for their outdoor shots, here on these cliffs, before decamping for Hollywood.

A slow wind blouses the tips of my hair. Buses from the Port Authority, chugging from the Lincoln Tunnel, accelerate along Boulevard East. Across the river Manhattan shimmers. A watery diesel scent of the Hudson gusts upward. Lights from a tugboat sprinkle the water, waves rippling beneath the cliffs of Weehawken. A classic Jersey setting: *All right, Mr. DeMille, I'm ready for my close-up!*

Ready to be immortalized.

3.

I flip through a collection of historic New Jersey postcards. One, a sketch of the Bothwell, an Atlantic City beach hotel, features bathing beauties on the boardwalk. What the card doesn't show are its charred remains, burned in 1924. A portion of its casino on the steel pier remained intact, however, its luck only partially lost.

According to postcards circa 1950s, New Jersey's luck returns in the area of retail. The Bergen Mall Shopping Center, built in 1958, features sixty-three stores (including Stern's and J. J. Newberry's), with a weekly traffic count of between 155,000 and 220,000 people.

Garden State Plaza, built around the same time and located at the intersection of Route 17 and Route 4, features Bamberger's, self-described as "the world's largest shopping center." Every Christmas the Plaza's giant outdoor Santa Claus, more than five stories tall, greets shoppers from his chimney perched high above the parking lot.

Of course the information contained on the postcards is only true for back then.

Today New Jersey boasts approximately seventy malls, one even named Hamilton, after Alexander, I assume. It's a modern historical marker with more visitors, no doubt, than those paying respects at his isolated grassy remembrance on the Palisades.

Other postcards from the '50s feature the Swiss Chalet restaurant in Ramsey, an American flag flying out front, never to be mistaken for a café in Geneva. Its architecture is virtually indistinguishable from the pure Jersey Arcola Motor Lodge in Paramus, with forty identical brick cottages featuring steam heat. The baths are tiled (*sterilized for your protection*). Call HAckensack 3-9744 for reservations.

Over the years, as New Jersey evolves into the most densely populated state, malls come and go, are upgraded. Swiss Chalets are reincarnated into Olive Gardens, and motor lodges into Super 8 Motels.

Only the pristine postcards remain frozen in time, as things once were, preserved in glassine paper. They're lovingly stored in dark, dry drawers, thus able to withstand the vagaries of weather, bad luck, and time, regardless whether what they depict is now defunct or not.

I both remember various malls and restaurants as they appear in the postcards and don't. Memory is a form of hiraeth, a homesickness for a place that never quite exists the way it seemed at the time. Memory is also like time-elapsed photography revealing a different angle, a different view of Jersey—of me—every time I look.

4.

I walk down Rock Road in Glen Rock carrying my plastic transistor radio. It's encased in black leather, cutouts for dials, one round wheel for volume, the other spinning stations seeking the perfect song for just this moment. Music arrives from New York City, home of deejay Cousin Brucie, vaulting over skyscrapers, bubbling across the Hudson River, swooshing over the cliffs of the Palisades. By the time rock 'n' roll reaches me, one small Jersey girl, a mere speck in the universe, I feel a whirl of sound cycloning around me, propelling the backs of my knees as I walk familiar—though now no longer ordinary—suburban hometown streets. I pass Mandee's Dress Shop and Gilroy's Market. I stare into the plate-glass window of the Bake Shoppe, holding that sweet, sweet music close to my ear.

5.

I sit in the back seat of the Plymouth, my parents in front, as we pass Fair Lawn, Cedar Grove, Verona. We drive through suburban towns, all the main streets with their shops selling clothes and gifts: a Peoples Bank on this corner, an Esso service station on another. We cross railroad tracks that, Monday through Friday, funnel dads into Manhattan, while moms drive their kids to school. I am mesmerized by the swish of car tires, by the overpowering sameness, the stillness, the hopefulness. We appear as ordinary as the day.

But are we?

Does that which is domesticated balance the wild and untamed? Or simply mask it? Where—what—are potential ruptures in the sameness of days?

A woman stands on a curb waiting for our car to pass. Her hat is yellow, the color of caution. A sign, a portent, a warning I fail to heed.

6.

At a Glen Rock block party, the deejay plays one 45 RPM record after another, spinning like planets in a rockin' universe. Bobby Vinton's "Blue Velvet," Buddy Holly's "That'll Be the Day," Frankie Valli and the Four Seasons' "Big Girls Don't Cry," Ricky Nelson's "Travelin' Man," Dion's "Runaround Sue," Leslie Gore's "It's My Party."

Other than music, the town is quiet. Night permeates Glen Rock with the everlasting memoried scent of chlorine from swimming pools and vanilla from the Nabisco plant on the edge of town.

7.

During the same party, I hold my boyfriend Jamie's hand: Jamie, with dimples and freckles, golden hair pale as sunrise dusting his forearms. The theme to *A Summer Place* plays. We dance. I want to believe this warmth will last into autumn, winter, spring.

8.

Years and years after high school graduation, I see Jamie again, a planned reunion. He returns me to that younger Glen Rock "me," to soft summer days lying beside each other on a blanket by the public swimming pool. Our skin smells of coconut oil, a still snapshot of safety, calm and warm, as if nothing has changed—or nothing *will* change. Ever. If only we remained beside each other encapsulated in time, days scented of blue hydrangeas, heavenly as dew.

If only.

9.

How can you not feel venustation for sugary, rhythmic, long-lasting New Jersey summery days? Don't happy, honeyed people live longer? Maybe even forever?

But New Jersey "contains multitudes." Walt Whitman died in Camden, so he should know. It echoes voices of venustation and anvenustation from stuttering neon sounds of Route 17, to swishing silt of the shore, to the guttural clang of the Turnpike, to dark silences of the pine barrens, to whispering grassy leaves of North Jersey, to fiery cities. Ocean waves, to suburban honeysuckle, to city dusk. Every town has its own vocabulary from Cape May to Glen Rock to Newark. The words of each, just like cruising Route 17, propel their own unflinching narratives.

Voices—some beautiful, some not—ascend and descend in New Jersey's simmer.

Just like my fate.

10.

One Friday afternoon, several hours before I encounter a man beneath the boardwalk, I drive down shore to South Jersey to my family's summer cottage. I pull into the driveway. I pluck the key from beneath the front mat. Inside I turn on a faux-Tiffany lamp and toss my purse, a proto-hippie cloth satchel, onto the couch. It contains maybe ten dollars, pearly lipstick, a package of Sen-Sens. The shuttered room smells of ocean and seaweed. Against the far wall is a fireplace, cinders mixing with must. I rattle the warped windows open. I kick the door ajar though the latch on the screen door is broken.

Should I have seen that as an omen? That latches should be fixed. That girls should not prowl the boardwalk—or maybe even Route 17—alone. Especially at night. Do I miss or misinterpret the signs, the metaphors, the symbols, the foreshadowing?

Later, in my white Keds sneakers, I walk the boardwalk to the carnival awash in the taste of Fralinger's salt-water taffy, peanut brittle, cotton candy. I sit on a wood bench on the boardwalk overlooking the Atlantic. South Jersey: the salty scent of ocean and pine barrens. Tinny music from the carousel—surely it's Sinatra, Jersey's own, "Are You Lonesome Tonight" or "Body and Soul"—croons over summer crowds. The wood horses revolve around and around, night after night, never wavering from their preordained route.

If only *I* never wavered, never stood up. . . .

If only I never left that wood bench to walk down the steps onto the sand. The waxing night below the boardwalk, beneath it, is deserted. Except for one knife-thin man.

11.

After that night I suffer my own form of alalia—an inability to speak certain specific words. I label this personal censorship because no one, including me, wants to hear them. Initially, I tell no one about the knife-thin man under the boardwalk or its aftermath. Decades pass before *these* words are resurrected—recovering from this one moment—a searing flash of death, which, against all odds, I survive.

12.

But for now a star flames across space before it's extinguished, sizzling into the ocean. Lights from the Ferris wheel create a night not too dark, not too black. Unlike stars or people, these lights, if they burn out, are easily replaced with new bulbs.

13.

Everything always happens—in all time, for better or worse—and always in New Jersey.

MISS ROUTE 17
REFUSES TO GROW OLD

anabiosis: return to life after apparent death

For example: "I experience anabiosis
listening to Adam Lambert sing."

Adam Lambert, framed in a spotlight, rises, as if levitating, onto a platform at the rear of the stage. He wears a feathered top hat, fringed jacket, black pants, boots. His sequins and glitter sparkle. I stand three rows back from the stage but not close enough. To gain an inch or two of elevation, I jam my foot between the spokes of the wheelchair of an elderly woman who earlier, deliberately, left the adjacent barrier-free section and rolled into me, poking me in an attempt to get me to move, which I did not.

For balance I gently lean against the shoulder of the young guy wedged on my right, whom I befriended, while waiting for the concert to start. Now the woman doesn't even notice I'm perched on the wheel, albeit only briefly.

This is one of those moments when looking back on the choices I made, I will wonder, *What the fuck was I thinking?*

But now, in Adam's presence, we are cloaked in a black-magic trance, a malarial fever, an outbreak of frenzied worship. Adam is quinine or, no, *he* is the fever spiking behind our foreheads. With one smile at the audience, he slowly struts down the steps of the platform. That smile is as seductive as an occluded star at twilight when you know, if you wait long enough, clouds will part. Steam rises as if from a mystical bayou—or rises from Adam himself—or rises from me, from all of us. As Adam sings, a viscous blue light descends as if from a voodoo moon.

Earlier, we fans waited hours outside the Royal Oak Theater in suburban Detroit. Only general admission tickets were sold, no seats, assigned or otherwise. So in order to be close to the stage, to Adam, I arrive at 4:30 p.m., from my home in West Michigan, securing a place in line, even though the doors don't open until 8:00 p.m. The line streams around the block on the scorching sidewalk jammed with tween girls, middle-aged women, gay guys, and straight men with dates. Many are dressed for this Glam Nation Tour. One little girl wears a frilly polka-dot dress with a pink sash, pink earrings, a pink boa, and tennis shoes resembling combat boots. Middle-aged women wear rhinestone tops, tight pants, and five-inch heels. One carries a purse laminated with Adam's photograph. In the hour after hour of heat, all the hyped makeup, which Adam would surely appreciate if he could see it, which he can't, melts onto the sidewalk.

Two girls on line in front of me display handmade signs: "Adam I ♥ you."

I ♥ Adam, too, but I wear practical shorts, a cotton shirt, sensible shoes. On my head is a red-and-white striped cap to protect me from sunstroke. Adam-stroke. But I ♥ him enough to stand on the sidewalk for three and a half hours, ♥ him enough to make a beeline into the mosh-pit area once the doors open, ♥ him enough to stake a claim to my tiny piece of real estate, secure my spot, here in the third row of packed bodies.

"I'm not even going to clap for Allison or Orianthi." The young guy beside me refers to the two opening acts. The one, Allison Iraheta, is a former *American Idol* contestant, like Adam. "I don't want to mess up my hair."

"It looks very nice." I motion toward his hair sleek with product, streaked with red, a streak Adam would ♥ if he sees it, which he won't.

"Thank you," he says, relieved, patting the strands to ensure they remain in place.

This is the point in the evening, before the concert begins, when the elderly woman in the wheelchair rolls across a line taped on the floor, into my section. She tries to push me out of her way—though I'm not in her way. She wants a better view of the stage even though, before the show, it is deserted, save for a drum set. Her daughter comes over to calm her. A security guard instructs the woman to return to her own section. Thankfully the situation is resolved. Adam sings about love and tolerance. Perhaps the woman and I will ♥ each other *after* the show. For now, the backs of my knees are weak and sweaty. I've eaten only a peanut butter and grape jelly sandwich for dinner. I've waited hours, or seemingly decades, to see Adam Lambert. The ♥ wants what the ♥ wants.

In an interview, Adam explains how his concerts reflect "a New Orleans voodoo tribal psychedelic rock extravaganza inspired by mystique, fortune tellers, black magic, feathers. It's done with a smile and a wink to the audience, and it's witchy."[1]

A reporter tells Adam that the crowd for his New York City concert arrived the night before to claim their spaces in line. One woman traveled from New Zealand. People are adorned with Glam Nation makeup and platform shoes. Adam smiles and waves his hands, Goth with black nail polish. His eyeliner is *Smolder*, his cologne Dior's *Homme* scented with ginger, cedar, and sandalwood. The tattoo on his wrist is the Eye of Horus projecting light and energy, the energy flowing from Adam to his fans, from his fans back to Adam.

Now the spotlight follows Adam toward the front of the stage. He sings "Voodoo," then "Down the Rabbit Hole," and I follow him *down down down*. The guy beside me grabs my hand. I squeeze back. We grin at each other. The love on his face toward Adam is heartbreaking. He styled his hair preparing for Adam as if for a date. Earlier I learned he lives in Livonia, outside Detroit, and I imagine his life devoid of glamour and color until *Adam, Adam, Adam.* We both proclaim our love for Adam. Who ♥'s him more? "I drove over three hours to get here," I say.

"You must be very devoted," he replies.

Devoted? Or released from a smudge of midlife, from a sleepless sleep, awakening, startled, as if I'm still (or never stopped?) listening to my teenaged rock 'n' roll while cruising gritty Route 17. Has nothing, no music, seduced me since? All grown up now, I listen to Adam's CD *For Your Entertainment* nonstop whenever I drive around in my yuppie Toyota RAV 4.

I bought the RAV in the first place because, shrinking into middle age, I had trouble seeing over the dashboard of my previous car. It felt low to the ground; *I* feel low to the ground, succumbing to invisibility. Besides, driving my previous car with standard transmission, I found it difficult to shift gears, given the touch of arthritis in my knee.

Now I'm adrift in red-and-green lasers spearing the air like flaming arrows. My senses themselves surge from the cement floor up to the ceiling of the theater domed like a temple or a cathedral, higher still, rocketing in space. I am rising above my body awash in billions of molecules of more than seventeen hundred screaming and swooning fans all inhaling Adam Lambert.

Adam is delicious, translucent, wet . . . a strutter with kohl deepening blue-blue eyes dazzling as stained-glass crystal. His voice is naked as water, holy as prayer, a ghost-y growl, perfume, incense, scotch . . . sacred and porous as animal bone, slow as beach clouds, sacrificial.

His voice soars across night on shooting stars that pierce your heart with heat, with ice, with darkness, with light. Each note seeps around panes of winter windows warming frost that shivers the cusp of midnight. Hearing Adam Lambert sing is like New Year's Eve on Saturn with all the rings and moons on red alert.

Truly, I don't know what all these words mean either. Adam surpasses vocabulary, grammar, punctuation. We're talking fan here, as in *fanatic*.

When Adam sings "Whole Lotta Love," I am jolted by crushed mint, the taste of fantasy. *He stares straight into my eyes.* Really, I'm not kidding, he does!

The first time I saw Adam on television, on *American Idol*, past and present collided as if psychedelic clothes, gnawed by moths, were suddenly rewoven, made anew. Watching him, I'm *his* age again—neon bright, no longer shadowy—hippie-ing my way once again into love beads, dangly earrings, tie-dye, miniskirts before they were ironic or retro. In short, he embodies the sexual, political, androgynous cultural explosion of the 1970s. Adam wears the costumes *we* used to wear. He decorates himself as I once did. He even claimed *he* wanted "to be a hippie" after appearing in an overseas production of *Hair*.[2] With Adam, I resurrect my younger, flower-child self. Morph her into my middle-age self.

And for the teeny-bopper girls in the audience, girls too young to drive: Don't they also love his sequins and costumes and makeup? Don't little girls love to play dress-up, too?

For women, whether middle aged or tweens, since he is gay, he is a *safe* dangerous man. He raises an eyebrow and dares you to do whatever he asks . . . or whatever *you* ask of yourself. I first heard Adam sing the hard-rocking "Whole Lotta Love" on *American Idol*. When it ended, his innocent grin acknowledged the applause: still a boy in search of love even in a silver-studded jacket. From boy to man to gay to flamboyance to androgyny to whiplash-smart entertainer, to pure honesty, when he explains how he wants to bring people together to celebrate similarities not differences, even as he believes "it's a really, really cool thing to be able to show people that you can be proud of yourself and never make apologies for it."[3] He takes risks. He doesn't play it safe. "Own your walk," he says.[4]

How wise when he asserts the need for both inclusivity and individ-

uality; how tenderly naive when he uses the phrase "really, really cool."
Although if someone else were to say that, I'd roll my eyes. Maybe his
1970s ideal, urging us all to love one another, to embrace all sides of
ourselves, is hokey. Yet true. And he sings it so well.

Now as he stares straight into my eyes (I'm *still* not kidding), his gaze
causes me to make one small gesture. So far I've not waved my arms,
sung aloud with the audience, or shouted his name. Perhaps I still
feel as if adulthood requires decorum. Or maybe I'm too tranced by
Adam even to breathe. Almost unaware I now, however, touch the bill
of my cap with my forefinger. To acknowledge him? Acknowledge a
connection—this longing—which he might appreciate if he recognizes
it. Which he won't. It's not a baseball cap. Rather, it's reminiscent of
the peaked caps once sported by the Beatles. I haven't worn it in years.
Why tonight? Before leaving home I hadn't planned my wardrobe, only
thought I'd need a hat for protection from the sun. This candy-striped
one is a tribute to adolescence, youth.

   I don't recall when I bought it. I doubt I owned it when I attended
a Beatles concert at DC Stadium. Why bother? I sat light-years away
from them in the bleachers. They would never notice me or a cap. I
couldn't really hear or see them either. I don't remember what they
looked like in person or which songs they sang. That concert, like the
past itself, is distant.

   Or, no, *not* distant.

   I hear Adam sing as if I am still in high school, rock and rolling in
teenage hangouts, cruising Route 17 in that v-8 Plymouth, a car Adam
would surely love if only he could have driven with me. His voice is
like fiery blasts of Jersey. That urgent *thwang* of metal ricocheting off
metal . . . cigarette smoke seductively webbing neon . . . when I *was, was,
was* a girl who loved all those teenaged boys, their black hair slicked
like Adam's hair *now* . . . jukebox evenings as powerful as Adam's voice
years before he was born.

   Here, tonight, do I want *that* past back? Well, I want *a* past—

youth—in order to magically merge into a new improved me. I long for the freedom of that gold-finned Plymouth, back when I sweated through summer on hot vinyl seats. I feel suspended between the age of that woman in the wheelchair and Adam's youth. Which is stronger? I glance at the woman. Even in the exploding music, she's drifted asleep.

More than anything, I now realize, the woman scares me. No. The woman's *age* scares me. Earlier, when I looked at her, I envisioned myself—a "self" I never want to be. I taste pale gray shame in the back of my throat. If only I could sing, even my regrets would be beautiful.

Adam's gaze glides away from me. But I want to believe—I *do* believe—I hold onto his timelessness, his never-ending *now*. I must stand in the same equatorial coordinates as Adam even for a moment. Or forever.

In short, pre-Adam, I slumped into middle age. But now he and his music jump-start my heart better than any defibrillator. I want to wake up the woman. We both must absorb the concert to keep us grooving as long as possible.

Next Adam appears on stage wearing a leather vest. His shoulders are bare. Freckles, small and tender, seemingly shy, float on pale skin amidst dark heat and glitter. All this and a voice that propels you, yes, *you*, from tender freckles to campy hype to smoldering sexuality to tranced beatitude. He's the boy-next-door-black-leather-rocker who isn't afraid of lace. He sings of pain and joy and loneliness and peace and love and sexuality and freedom.

My feelings toward him aren't particularly sexual. They are deeper. I want to evanesce inside his body, zip myself up in his skin, in his veins, in his incense and essence, in order to absorb his vibrations against every cell in my body. He fills his own body with a masculine primitive raw and tender heart. I want the power of that heart, too.

Of course women love him. Unlike most (straight) guys, he's in touch with his feelings—and don't you dare question my pop-psych analysis. He sings of self-empowerment, offers relationship advice between songs, makeup advice in interviews. Don't all of us women in the audience feel as if we suppress some of who we are in order to live in a world still run by straight men? If so, are we women—and even some straight men—in the audience all going gay for Adam Lambert? Do we all release our gay other/inner selves to join anima with animus? Yin with yang? Polka-dot dresses with combat boots?

Everyone in the audience thinks they have a personal relationship with Adam. The woman in the wheelchair. The tweens screaming behind me. The guy who smooths his hair over and over. "I'm going to wait outside by his bus after the concert," he whispers to me.

At midnight I find myself outside on a wet, puddled sidewalk. During the concert a storm gusted through, knocking small branches off trees, a storm we never heard inside the thundering theater. The audience, admiring their newly purchased CDs and concert T-shirts, whooshes past me. Adam's tour bus hums in the parking lot waiting to rumble to the next gig.

I stand beneath the dark marquee. The sign, not yet changed for the next concert, still announces "Adam Lambert, Fri., 8." *Always* announcing "Adam Lambert."

I clutch the T-shirt I purchased. Adam appears bold and silver against a black background. His topaz eyes, edged with black, stare fiercely between his fingers spread wide across his face. Each fingernail is black, the fingers themselves studded with silver-chained jewelry. Below, in pink script, are the words *For Your Entertainment*.

Adam, *his* essence, *is* balanced between anima and animas. Yin and yang. Full of grace. I will never be like him, yet he returns me to *me,* balances the current me with the teenage girl who once was fearless of fate.

Adam offers a voice that understands the *now-ness* of life, more than the *then-ness* of death—understands the ease and power of living.

I follow a trail of drenched sequins to my RAV, where I sit on the leather seat. I listen to *For Your Entertainment* following Adam's voice, his glitter, the past, the future, the masks he conjures, all the way backward, home, as well as forward and beyond. . . .

. . . following an otherworldly Adam Lambert, believing in the eternity of the soul, or believing that The Three Fates will lengthen the thread of the life of my soul, if not that of my body. Or maybe The Fates will allow me to have an out-of-body experience while still residing *in* my body. If so I bless them for this.

My only out-of-body experience pre-Adam occurred shortly after graduating college, visiting the Cathedral of Notre Dame. Upon entering, my hurried tourist feet slowed. For a moment I couldn't move. My eyelids, my palms, my bare shoulders flushed from the rose stained-glass windows—this cathedral that "shines out like the sun among stars."[5]

I lowered myself onto a pew. At first I felt the weight of the Gothic towers, the lateral vaults, the large cross separating the choir from the nave. The bells. The organs. The weight of religion itself, windows depicting saints, martyrs, virgins, angels, the Savior—stars shining on the wounds on his hands—temple lamps lit around him.

An elderly woman sat in the next pew. A black shawl covered her hair, her palms pressed in prayer.

I had no prayers. I didn't know any. But I couldn't leave.

And yet I left . . .

While I sat there it's as if I levitated from my body, my soul rising straight out of my skin, soaring beyond the flying buttresses to become one with an ethereal existence. I entered the stained-glass windows, my soul awash in the blue, gold, red of the Flight to Egypt, the Annunciation, the Descent into Hell, the Temptation of Eve, of Eve and Adam, *oh, Adam* . . . me, the thinnest crease of light, smaller, yet larger, than I've ever been before. So as I lifted myself away from my self, away from the wood pew, I mystically became more of my self, felt a deeper sense of my self—*an everlasting forever me*—a feeling I've never had before or since until . . .

Yes, *I know, I know*: Comparing an Adam Lambert concert to a religious experience in the Cathedral of Notre Dame is too much. Comparing his voice to the power of a V-8 Plymouth engine is too much. To imagine Adam as a supernova among stars or a moon among suns is too much. To imagine the freckles on his shoulders like pin-pricks of stained-glass light is too much. Comparing him to the roar of that Plymouth *and* a religious hallucination—all in one fell swoop, at one and the same time—is *definitely* too much.

I touched the peaked bill of my hippie cap in tribute; the young man beside me stroked his hair; the old woman in the Cathedral of Notre Dame pressed her palms together in prayer: such small gestures for such enormous needs.

THE THREE FATES

How Much Is the Moon Worth?

This is a daily ponder, walking sun-infested streets, too clearly lit by day. Why, you might ask? Have we nothing better to accomplish or consider? Why yes! Yes we do! We oversee husks of what once was: people, animals, flora, fauna, lizards, arachnids, sea horses. Also pearls. The crushed spine of a book. How else to convey our spirits, sometimes troubled, sometimes not, by such lofty decisions. Our minds ease when we allow our skin to be refreshed by moonlight, or a most gentle breeze off the cliffs.

Otherwise, these husks . . .

Sleeping in doorways. Under bridges. Inside tunnels. Out in fields of potato farms.

There is no god or religion to save you. There is no "better place." We Three Fates control your Fate. Otherwise you are alone.

Death resembles *you*, wherever you currently reside. You take *your* Death with you when you go.

An empty sound conveys familiar terrain. An absent scent. Taste dries. Fingertips numb.

It is all directly before you, in front of you.

But not.

THE REMARKABLE
DEATH-DEFYING EXPLOITS
OF MISS ROUTE 17

swoopstake: in an indiscriminate manner

I. THE SEINE, THE CHARLES, THE STYX

One night as a college freshman in Boston, my three girlfriends and I wander deserted streets in Back Bay. We seek an address written on a scrap of crinkled paper: the apartment of a man who will pierce our ears. The address itself was whispered over the black pay phone on the fourth floor of the dorm. We only belatedly realize the doctor probably believes we're coming for an abortion, that he thought "ear piercing" was a euphemism. Which, in our case, it is not.

We ring the doorbell. Heavy footsteps. We each clasp a pair of gold studs in our fists. Our textbooks in green book bags are slung over our shoulders.

A woman who could be a nurse, although not dressed as one, answers the door.

We sit in a waiting room on a stained brocade sofa. A frayed Oriental carpet covers a wood floor. We expect to hear screams echoing down the hallway.

Girls who graduate from Glen Rock High School do not end up on a soiled couch in an abortionist's waiting room if they aren't pregnant. Or even if they are.

We file into his office. A few strands of hair slick his scalp. His white shirt is gray, his trousers wrinkled.

All four of us hold out our gold studs. He waves them aside. He says he'll insert his own silver ones that stay in for two weeks. Then we must return in order for him to remove his "starter" earrings and insert our gold ones.

My lobes go numb. A form of necrosis? Cells dissolving, shedding, dying. But then, slowly, I feel a small tingle. A faint slosh of life. A silvery, unaccustomed weight tugs the flesh.

Back then, sure, I worry about disease and death, but this Miss Route 17 girl also possesses pure teenage recklessness.

Besides, we are captured in a singular moment of history: long past the bubonic plague yet years before the AIDS epidemic or the outbreak of hepatitis C. We have evolved to the epoch of cleansing and sanitizing pierced ears even in back-alley abortion offices. Or we are devolving back to that.

For I also imagine the Charles River gloomy as the River Styx, a contagion transforming Boston from something bright and Charlesian into something dark and Stygian.

But for now we girls, training studs in place, leave his obscure street and rush toward Copley Square. The breeze off the water coils our ponytails, ruffles our plaid skirts. I am pure Jersey Girl yet, with the earrings, feel exotic, Parisian, as if I'm strolling along the Seine hand in hand with an older lover.

Instead we girls sit in a Friendly's ice cream shop spooning chocolate sundaes, nervous, as if we have done something illegal. We stare at ourselves, at each other, in plate-glass windows, turning our heads from side to side, adorned with tiny punctures piercing us forever. We look and look, wanting to see how we will appear for the rest of our lives. But we are unimaginative criminals. We can't even see who we are, to say nothing of what we might become.

2. LEANING INTO THE CURVE

Still a freshman in college, I leave early from a fraternity party at MIT. Those boys, those boys: predictably drunk. Loutish. I walk toward the

Massachusetts Avenue Bridge drifting in the freedom that no one in the world knows where I am right this second. I stand on the curb to hitchhike back to my dorm. I hold out my hand, my forefinger pointing down: *Stop here. Right now.* Cars speed past ruffling my cotton gypsy shirt with red-and-green embroidery. I've never lived alone in a big city. The energy dazzles my skin. Lights on the buildings sparkle the Charles until I myself feel ablaze.

A man on a motorcycle stops. He doesn't cut the engine. He nods his head toward the pillion, behind him. I slide on. He doesn't ask where I'm going. Nor do I tell him. In the roar of the engine we wouldn't hear each other anyway. He will deliver me to where he thinks I belong.

I clasp my arms around his white T-shirt. My hands rest on his leather belt looping his jeans. My own jeans are men's Levis. I don't remember where I found them though I didn't buy them new. Maybe I discovered them in a heap of clothes on the floor of some man's fraternity room. They ride low on my hips. I press my thighs against the man, my forehead against the nape of his neck. He smells dark and weedy, of diesel. No helmet. My long hair gusts around my head.

We cruise Back Bay along Dartmouth, Marlborough, Exeter . . . wherever the night opens up allowing passage. I've never before ridden on a motorcycle. Yet I automatically sway into the grace of his movements, defying gravity, stronger than physics. People on the sidewalks, other cars on the streets, all seem miniature and muffled beside the power of the motorcycle, its metal streaking the night black with freedom.

We speed over to the harbor. He cuts the engine. My body, my thighs, still throb to its roar even in the sudden silence. Especially in the sudden silence. He slides off the bike pulling me with him. My legs feel wobbly. I sit on a patch of grass. He pushes me back. He tugs the metal button on my perfect jeans, jeans I will wear for years until they're shredded thread.

I don't look at him. I stare past him, over his shoulder. I want to breathe deeply enough to inhale stars. The sky is white with them, like one night on the island of St. Croix, past midnight. I awake in a villa out in the country, on vacation with my parents and sister from our home on St. Thomas, before we move to New Jersey. I free my feet from the tangled mosquito net. I slip from bed. I gaze out screenless windows. The trade winds ruffle the sleeves of my pajamas. Waves *shush* the shore. A quarter moon casts a pale light across fever grass. Sugarcane fields smell of dark rum and brown sugar.

Over the crest of a hill gallops a white stallion: the sound that awakens me. His hooves smack limestone soil while his mane rises and falls like jets of white-hot flame. I grip the windowsill as if the swirl of air from the stallion will gust me outside. Or, still a little girl, maybe I hold the sill to prevent myself from rushing after him, grabbing tufts of mane to pull myself onto his back. He doesn't pause as he races past the window.

Then he is gone. It's as if, in his speed, he gallops straight off the earth and dollops of him now whiten the planets, the stars, the galaxies.

The motorcycle man bends low over me, his face close to mine.

Now, my breath no longer rushing, I struggle to breathe as if a slow hypoxia settles over my eyelids.

Only a year earlier, I struggle with that knife-thin man at the Jersey shore beneath the boardwalk. No stars that night, the sky blacked-out by the boardwalk.

Did that danger lead me to this one? Does one risk birth another?
Why hitchhike?
Why arise from that bench on the boardwalk and enter darkness below?

The motorcycle man bends low over me.

I don't want to be here, yet I stay. Why? I'm less alive here, my spine pressed cold against the ground, then in that long-ago, longed-for light.

UNTIL MY NUMBER COMES UP

I stand here waiting. To disappear or sing.

—Francesca Lia Block

Sucissive: spare hours, or time

1. *How much of human life is lost in waiting?*
RALPH WALDO EMERSON

I sit in the waiting room, though some would call it a gate area, in the Atlanta airport. I'm flying to Rochester, Minnesota, where my mother just died from lung cancer. I will meet my sister there to attend to the cremation. All the seats are taken. Suitcases, strollers, and parcels clog the aisles. I wish I could sit far away from crying babies, screeching toddlers. A gang of young men laugh boisterously, drunkenly.

Restless, I glance at the flight status board. Will the plane leave on time? Will I miss my connection in Minneapolis?

April sun radiates off the massive windows. Planes rush down the runway for takeoff. Others, after landing, glide up to gates.

The area seethes and buzzes. I feel suffocated, cramped.

I hold an unopened book in my lap. I can't read because it's noisy; I can't read because I check the flight status board every thirty seconds. I can't read because, although my mother wasn't a good mother, she was, still, *my* mother. I must comprehend the fullness of the loss.

Daily, thousands of passengers congregate in airport waiting areas: people on vacation, people abandoning or rekindling love, people fleeing to or from emergencies. Whole lives change in these anonymous spaces. Yet everyone seems distracted, oblivious to their surroundings, forgetting the real reason for their trips. How can they absorb the momentous events taking place?

Waiting rooms should provide decorum. To spend time in one is an activity in and of itself. It requires concentration in order to successfully depart, to leave here and to reach what lies beyond.

I realize, belatedly, it's noisier than usual because the NCAA basketball "Sweet Sixteen" playoffs are being held in Minneapolis. How can this happen at the same time as my mother's death? But that's the nature of random encounters with strangers in waiting rooms. We wash ashore in one particular place, one particular time, all heading to the same ultimate destination although for disparate reasons.

By the time the gate agent announces it's time to board, we're running more than a half-hour late. Once all the drunk basketball fans and parents with toddlers settle into seats, we're almost an hour behind schedule. I reach the gate for my connecting flight to Rochester just as the attendant closes the door to the Jetway.

"Please, can you let me on?" I ask. "My mother died."

She expresses condolences but says she's not allowed to open the door. The plane is ready to push back from the gate.

I feel stranded. I cry as if I *have* to make this connection even though my mother is already dead. Upon arrival in Rochester, I will only spend the night in her now-deserted apartment.

But I want to depart this waystation immediately. I need to escape.

2. *Every bad situation is a blues song waiting to happen.*
AMY WINEHOUSE

My sister and I sit in cushiony wingback chairs in the waiting room of the funeral parlor. On the end table is a cut-glass bowl of candy. My sister has been crunching one after another, while I've cradled the same lemon drop on my tongue for close to fifteen minutes. It's almost dissolved. Still, my mouth feels dry, my eyes drier. Who can mourn in a room that smells of formaldehyde or something like it—maybe mothballs? Maybe the desiccated scent of perfume that women wore in the 1940s.

I fold and unfold my candy wrapper as we wait for the funeral director to greet us.

The wait seems destined: I can neither rush it nor delay it.

The recycled air feels oppressively heavy, the dim lamplight dense as honey. It's difficult to breathe. The plush carpet absorbs all sound: no footsteps, no voices, no office machinery. No Muzak. No sudden screams from bodies springing to life.

Well thank god for that.

My sister and I decide to buy the least expensive canister for our mother's remains. My sister hates to spend money though she has a lot of it. I don't have much money, but I don't particularly care how much I spend. I just want it over with.

I want to be rid of the thought of my mother lying on a gurney covered with a white sheet no longer waiting for anything.

3. *Sitting quietly, doing nothing, spring comes,*
and the grass grows by itself. ZEN PROVERB

My parents, brother-in-law, and I sit in a Boston hospital waiting room. Well, my brother-in-law doesn't sit; he paces back and forth awaiting the arrival of his first child. My older sister labors in a different kind of waiting room, one imbued with magic, miracles, and luck. I can't imagine, *can't imagine* a fully formed human slipping out of another human being. I struggle to sit still then stand to look out the dark window. Tornadoes of swirling, thrashing snow virtually obliterate night. The view is also occluded by my own dim reflection superimposed over the immensity of the storm, the cosmic-ness of imminent creation.

My nephew is wheeled in. He's asleep in a clear plastic crib, his own waiting area. He's swaddled in a white coverlet, his arms free. I didn't know his fingernails would be so heartbreaking in their tiny clichéd cuteness. I press my own finger against the plastic as if I can touch him, but his cellular essence is beyond my reach. I press my finger harder. I whisper *Todd. Todd. Todd.* Can you hear me? The thin rise and fall of his chest: How has he learned to breathe all on his own so quickly? Does this mean he'll also know how to survive, to unravel the tangled vagaries of life?

4. *In one month alone, I lost three hours of this "human life"
dawdling in [doctor] waiting rooms.* LESLEY ALDERMAN

I sit on a green upholstered chair in my doctor's waiting room in Grand Haven, Michigan, having moved here from Georgia. Identical chairs line the walls with an extra row down the middle; really, this is two waiting rooms in one. I find a seat as far away from everyone as possible, and wish I could move farther still when someone coughs or sneezes, spewing germs. These rooms should be sterile and antiseptic, so going to the doctor doesn't mean courting disaster.

On the other side of the room an elderly man snores while his wife hovers beside him. As much as I don't want to die, I'm more afraid of becoming lost to old age. But unless I suddenly stroke out, I am waiting to grow aged, decrepit. Nevertheless, looking on the bright side, if I'm confined to a bed-on-wheels, I can always get up a head of steam and roll myself in front of an oncoming truck— before I lose my marbles, before I'm simply a bag of plasma and protein—still able, however, to argue with The Fates and insist this is all one big mistake.

A locked door leads to the examination rooms. I wonder what my doctor will tell me today during my annual physical: good news? Bad? As long as I'm in the waiting room I can hope for, anticipate, the best, though I always expect the worst.

A nurse opens the door. She calls my name.

I cross the floor to my fate leaving my fellow travelers—sick, prognosis unknown—behind.

5. *Waiting . . . / for the secret of eternal life to be discovered.*
LAWRENCE FERLINGHETTI, "I AM WAITING"

My first appointment with the hypnotist, near my house in Michigan, is on Halloween. I sit in his clinic at 6:45 p.m. in the deserted waiting room, waiting for his previous client—trying to exorcise her own demons—to leave. Even the receptionist is gone for the day. Through a glass partition I'm able to see down the hall. All the wood doors for the therapists' offices are closed. I'm fifteen minutes early.

On one wall hangs a quilt, on another a large oil painting of springtime flowers. Both seem to have been here a long time. A clock hangs on the wall behind me, so I have to turn around to see the time. A sound system plays classic rock 'n' roll: "You Are My Destiny," "Travelin' Man," "Stop! In the Name of Love." Touchstones from my teenage years echo.

At 7:10 I worry I have the wrong day, the wrong hour, that my hypnotist won't walk down that corridor to greet me. The building seems deserted. I hear nothing from behind the glass partition.

The hypnotist also specializes in mind-body therapy, including biofeedback. I don't fully understand his type of therapy, but, generally speaking, I believe a connection exists between mind and body. I'm here because I fear my own personal connection is damaged. Like right now, my body feels a ribbon of anxiety ripple from the base of my neck to my knees. The rational side of my mind tells me that the hypnotist *will* open the glass door and fix me. The irrational side tells me I'll sit here forever, unfixed, listening to classic rock 'n' roll.

I guess there are worse fates.

I wonder what the hypnotist's office looks like. I anticipate whether I'll like him. Will he like me? Will he think he can help me and accept me as a client? What's the first question he'll ask? Will I feel scared to talk with him? How can I explain to him my fear of death?

The waiting room vibrates with anticipation.

I could post a Facebook update using my iPhone: "Waiting to see a hypnotist." But that would interrupt my intense focus of watching for the hypnotist to open the door. The most important job to perform in a waiting room, after all, is waiting.

Later, once I reach his office, I will understand the job that's required of me is to be hypnotized.

The space *between* the waiting room and his office is uncharted territory. During those few moments I'm in a state of transit: neither here nor there. What's supposed to happen in that corridor, that no-man's land? As months pass, as I continue to see the hypnotist, I will come to understand that we never speak when we're between these two points: the *here* and the *there*.

Waiting in a waiting room can be sacred, but only if you banish to oblivion all that is not *of* the waiting room.

6. *I'm so tired, tired of waiting.* THE KINKS

I sit on a hard plastic chair in the waiting room designated for the Toyota service department. I received a recall notice on my RAV 4, something about the rear lower suspension and whether a wheel alignment was performed using a proper torque specification. If not, backlash developing at the threaded portion of the arm, followed by formation of rust, could result in loss of control of the vehicle.

Sudden death, I think, though the recall notice does not suggest this.

The RAV 4 will also undergo a tune-up: oil changed, filters replaced, tires checked for pressure. The car should be good to go.

The waiting room smells of rubber, paint, and stale potato chips. The TV blasts an early-morning game show. On one side of me a man talks on his cell phone. On the other, a woman digs in a box of vending-machine candy while reading an old issue of *People*. Another man does *this*. Another woman *that*. We are a strange conglomeration of humanity, Fellini-film extras, with nothing in common except sitting together awaiting our cars, currently in various states of existential disrepair.

I'm faced with the trite but nonetheless frightening thought that life itself is a waiting room: waiting for breakfast, for school to start, for marriage or divorce. Waiting for an airplane to depart, for a concert to begin, for a parent to die, for a phone call with bad news, for an email with good news. *Waiting, waiting, waiting* at the grocery store checkout line, for a doctor's appointment that will either cure me or end my waiting once and for all. Waiting for a therapist's appointment that will only intensify my sense of loss and regret. Waiting for my body to fall apart.

After an hour the Toyota service manager approaches me. I'm sure he's going to tell me that my car is a contagion of fluidy leaks, undercarriage rust, that the vehicle won't make it out of the repair shop as far as the street. Instead he smiles and says the repair work is complete. The rear-wheel alignment won't suddenly and catastrophically unalign itself. I won't (immediately, anyway) die in a fiery explosion.

I slide onto the leather seat. Carefully, religiously, I click in my seat belt. I check both ways for oncoming traffic. I maneuver into the proper lane. No burning rubber, no squealing out into hazardous traffic. I set the cruise control for the posted speed limit. Well, okay, a couple of miles per hour over. Without the security of a waiting room, you're next on tragedy's list.

> 7. *People are always saying, we must wait, we must wait.*
> *What are we waiting for?* JAMES BALDWIN

I sit in the waiting room at Lakeshore Dermatology Laser & Medical Spa. I'm here to have a basal cell spot scraped off my nose. Surreptitiously I study faces, hands, whichever body parts are visible. What tumorous growth lurks behind the bandage on that woman's neck? What once sprouted on that man's cheek where a scar now trails beside his nose?

Two doors lead away from this waiting room. The door to the left is the dermatology unit. Enter here and you risk a diagnosis of basal cell, squamous cell, melanoma, and who knows what other kinds of cancer rooting inside a seemingly innocent-looking birthmark?

The door to the right leads to the spa where you're offered Megapeels, Biomedic-massages, photo-rejuvenation, laser therapy, micro-dermabrasions, liposculpture.

I watch as my fellow denizens of purgatory are called to their fate: right or left.

"My Sweet Lord" by George Harrison, who died of cancer, plays softly on the sound system.

In the middle of the waiting room is a display rack of hats to protect skin from harmful UV rays. Most are big, floppy, seemingly designed to protect your whole body. I try one on. It's unfashionable. Do you have to be frumpy to be healthy? But another one catches my eye: a straw cowgirl-style hat decorated with a string of turquoise-colored beads. I try it on and look at myself in the rack's little mirror.

I will leave here with just a small gouge in my nose and a hat for the remaining trail ahead, having dodged yet another bullet. But I know there's one out there, snug in some metaphorical cylinder of some metaphorical gun, waiting patiently. It's going to have to find me, though. I will wait for a lot of things, but not for that.

No.

I plan to keep moving forward even when I'm sitting still.

REQUIEM FOR A QWERTYIST

abditive: remote, secret, hidden

For example: "Surely one way to outsmart
death is by deciphering abditive messages in
mementos, keepsakes, paintings, or even
in everyday belongings simply left behind."

After rummaging around in a drawer of a desk I inherited from my mother, I'm unable to close it. I yank it out. A sheet of Carter's Midnight typewriter carbon paper sticks to the drawer's runners. Although wrinkled and crimped, the paper still shimmers with decorative silver stars floating among silver-ringed Saturns cascading across a black carbon universe. Wands of light radiate from each star. I hold the paper toward the window of my home office in West Michigan: a dark rectangle against light. The center of the paper is a worn palimpsest of letters and words. Only the borders, unstruck by typewriter keys, remain shiny.

I want to decode these ghostly words. Maybe I'll discover secrets about my mother, secrets I thought she packed and carried with her to the beyond. What did she fail to tell me about her life that she wants me to know now in her hereafter? Surely my mother hid this missive for me to discover only after she died.

I examine worn lines of type through a magnifying glass. Mainly it's a blur, impossible to shave one letter from atop the next in order to distinguish individual words and sentences. The paper itself is punctured, or punctuated with pinholes, a result of the period key striking over and over. All I decipher are a few words at the top of the page flush along the left-side margin, aligned like a poem.

EXCEPTIONAL lsjnriqjjkziixdjl;"
on gas
don't forget
slowly three times
start ignition with
very slight pressure on
let meter
bring back to original
Fay Silverman
911
Weehawken
865–059

To whatever the word "exceptional" refers must truly have been exceptional, highlighted, as it is, in capital letters. But the mélange of inscrutable letters that follows remains an unsolved mystery. Next, in lines two through eight, I see in my mind's eye the yellow Opal automobile my parents gave me. My mother typed the operating procedure, a residue of which remains on the carbon paper. Starting the car—in order for it not to stall out—required a mystical set of steps be performed both before and after cranking the ignition. Years later, when I sold the car, I also provided typed instructions to the buyer. I wonder if the car still runs. How many owners have been novitiates in the gnostic, otherworldly ritual required to bring the car to life: pump the gas pedal, flick the turn signal, silent prayers issued to carburetors and spark plugs. And, in return, blessings from gods for a foreign chariot the color of the sun.

The last four lines are handwritten in my mother's cursive script. Her name along with partial address and phone number—embedded in carbon—can never be erased.

I wouldn't have remembered the phone number on my own but now, even with one numeral smudged, it easily trips off my tongue.

Both my parents are dead. Yet I consider calling to see if they answer—just in case. Maybe your phone number belongs to you forever, can be forwarded to outer space or six feet under or wherever.

I always save contact information of deceased friends in my address book: two from brain aneurisms; two from traffic accidents; one from a rafting trip. A few suicides. Murders. Three friends died from cancer. My former therapist, Randy, died of heart failure in his early fifties. His email address was impath@aol.com. No, it still *is* impath@aol.com. I want to send a message there as if cyberspace is a new kind of heaven, and email a new kind of prayer.

I grow up in St. Thomas, in the West Indies, where I learn to type on my mother's black metal Underwood. It perches on a table in the sitting room reached through high archways from the front parlor. On rainy days I type for hours though I don't yet know how to spell many words. Undeterred, I fill page after page with lines such as wieheike aidnapew z owothes, ... theiw thelwppppwjwjet qpzqqzzzxx()()( ) „mxk wbv eiet 4opi;.?adfuz)l tiehw wil23445 5oi 988** ** **&&&&&###$$$%%%ai !!1? sgh rwe nclk???siehtie wooiejsu . . .

This appears to be gibberish now. But who's to say these letters and symbols don't contain urgent messages from my third-grade mind? Perhaps this rush of private words boiling across paper, spreading like an ink stain, are exactly the right ones in order to slip through pinhole-sized punctuation marks on pieces of carbon paper, apertures or portals to reach an everlasting *somethingness*. I imagine lm.pljui exploding past galaxies to black holes in outer space before slamming to the end of a sentence, where jdiwjNNN@@ beams white as the moon, or where cryptic ioegxnl remains embedded in carbon for future civilizations to decipher.

Summer vacations, my family departs St. Thomas to visit my Aunt Patsy and Uncle Esar in New York City. Mornings, I curl up like a cat on the wine-red carpet in my uncle's home office. A rhomboid of sunlight warms me. From this angle I mainly watch his sockless feet in cracked-leather slippers, while I listen to him type on his own Underwood. He writes jokes for a living. One by one he scrolls three-by-five-inch index cards into the platen. One joke per card, he tells me. Later in the day he lets me sit on his lap. He smells comforting, redolent of rye toast and orange pekoe tea. He places my small index finger on a particular key to help him type. I press down. The skin beneath my nail whitens with the pressure. *Tap.* He moves my finger to another letter. *Tap.* I wonder if the letters, the words, the jokes reside in my uncle's fingertips (mine?), not fully understanding the relationship between fingers and mind.

He doesn't get angry if my finger slides off a key hitting the wrong one by mistake. He unrolls the card and erases the error with a small rubber instrument that resembles a pinwheel with an attached brush. As he erases he inevitably sweeps away bits of the card. A ghostly image of the wrong letter still clings to it. The paper is rough where the rubber snagged it. Nevertheless he rolls the card back in the typewriter and strikes the correct letter. It's almost as if he invented a new letter, the way the two hug, body to soul.

When my uncle takes a break, I linger in his office. It buzzes with all the words typed on cards until I think they swirl inside my head, as if I absorbed them. I poke in the cubbyholes in his desk, tiny womb-like drawers, to discover secrets inside: stacks of new index cards, rubber bands, stamps, stray buttons. Mints wrapped in cellophane. I'd love to suck on one but don't. They look too perfect, pristine, full of life. Other times I flip through the pages of his first book, *Esar's Comic Dictionary*, published by Doubleday before I'm born.

Now, my aunt and uncle deceased, I sit at my desk in Michigan (November 12, 2017) and open his book. I flip through the alphabetically arranged pages before stopping at "dead," then "death."

"Dead: What you have to be before some people will say it with flowers."

"Death: Nature's withdrawal from its battle with your doctor's treatment of your illness."

Could these have been the jokes I myself typed on his cards years ago? But what kind of cosmic joke is death?

While still living in St. Thomas, before I properly learn to type, I play the piano on an upright. I sit on the bench facing the wall, my back toward windows overlooking the verandah and the Caribbean. One of my mother's watercolor paintings hangs above the piano. Now, years after her death, it adorns the wall in my study. It portrays me, or a version of me, playing the piano.

I'm dressed in green in the painting. When I think of myself back then, however, I'm wearing red French madras. In the painting a cat curls up beside the piano bench. In real life one of our cats might sneak inside the house, but usually they roam our jungled yard. In the painting the walls are blue-green, the color of the sea. But that color is a flight of imagination because the actual walls of our house are tan and white. I perch on the piano bench, bare toes pressing cool brass pedals. My fingers hover on the keys ready for action.

Sheet music is propped against the stand. But since I can't read notes, my head angles away from it, both in the painting and in real life. I play solely by ear.

My mother's easel and watercolors are set in a sunny alcove between the living room and verandah. Here she can see both inside and out: cats, sky, sea, Charlotte Amalie—me at the piano. My mother paints in the same manner as I play—fancifully and untrained—no professional lessons.

My beloved piano is out of tune, warped by humidity. Termite tunnels crisscross the instrument causing small echoes whenever a key is pressed. The veneer bench is likewise almost hollow making the wood softer, more fragile. But the piano's condition enhances the sound, a sound that can only be mine, for which I'm grateful.

I can't imagine how you could formally study such legerdemain anyway . . . the way a song I hear on the radio channels from ears to fingers to keys to sound. My untrained fingers sweep the keyboard in search of calypso rhythms—the *pong-pong* of steel-drum bands. *Day-oh, daaay-oh* . . . I love show tunes as well, particularly the theme song to *Kismet*. I've never seen the movie but associate "A Stranger in Paradise" with myself, born in Washington DC, but now living in the tropics.

My fingers plunk keys until sound itself shimmers—the air conveying melodies of *my* island—just as my mother paints a vision of *her* island. It's as if I play the actual rustle of palm fronds, the endless *shushing* of waves. I grow muggy, druggy. Frogs shiver beneath bromeliads, skin emerald and damp. The world gusts through my skin until music appears blue, yellow, green, red. All this occurs when my fingers caress ivory keys conjuring sound.

During long tropical days my mother paints—I play—as if under a voodoo spell, a spell that might never end, which might keep me alive forever if I'm lucky.

Luck runs out.

We move from the West Indies to Glen Rock, leaving my charmed, albeit termite-riddled piano, behind. We purchase a brand-new shiny upright. Because of the expense, my mother forces me to take lessons even though she herself doesn't consider art classes. Nor does she have an alcove in our brick ranch house. Instead she sets her easel in our windowless basement refinished with linoleum floors, fluorescent light, and sheet-rocked walls. To her right is the furnace to keep us warm during frigid winters. To her left are the modern washer and dryer. No more hanging clothes outside in the Caribbean sun. She paints while waiting for clothes to wash and dry.

I go to Mrs. K's house for piano lessons. She provides a red-covered copy of *Thompson's Teaching Little Fingers to Play*. I struggle to follow her instructions. Her voice seems muffled by gray light seeping through windows. The radiators in her house clank. I would prefer to play *their* rhythm, interpret rattling pipes into the ponging of a steel drum. I hunch in a wool skirt and sweater. The back of my neck, exposed below my ponytail, feels too thin, too cool. It'll never support my head. My head will never support my mind. My mind will never support all these strange notes and these stranger directions.

Only when urged do I tentatively press an index finger on middle C. Before, I never knew its importance, never noticed that pianos contain eighty-eight keys.

"All the notes you need are right there." She points to the sheet music. "On the staffs."

I see only meaningless black dots precariously balancing on parallel lines. "If you hum it, I could play it," I whisper.

She doesn't answer.

Maybe she doesn't understand me any more than I understand her. She paces the floor, a metronome herself. I stare at the sheet music while she tries to seduce me with the vocabulary of music, the dialect of sound. The more she explains things like diatonic major and natural minor scales, the dimmer my mind grows. Before, in the West Indies, notes tumbled from my ears to my fingers . . . sound meandering the way I followed winding donkey trails up/down volcanic mountains. It was in this roundabout wandering, in the detours, where I discovered—not instruments defining life—but the black magic of the subconscious. Back then, the vibration of the felt-covered hammers plonking the strings traveled straight out of my body and beyond, as if I constructed a world, *my* world, with each strike of the hammer.

Now, notes seem too organized, like straight suburban streets: *Walk to this corner, turn left, and you will reach your destination.* I don't want to reach a destination, a definitive ending, a dead end, no place else to go.

Mrs. K, frustrated, orders me to sit up straight on the hard, termite-free bench. My spine feels rigid, almost paralyzed. My hands feel too weighted to move.

"You're a stubborn little girl, aren't you?" she says.

Past the piano I stare at Mrs. K's floral wallpaper. The pale flowers smell like December.

"You will perform in the spring recital, and you won't want to embarrass your parents," she says, "or me."

I prepare by forcing myself to read music and memorize keys. Mrs. K smiles when I play four-four time. When I cross hands. When I learn rests.

One afternoon, listening to my transistor radio in my bedroom, I hear "Autumn Leaves" sounding as colorful as Caribbean flowers. I never much noticed the leaves, themselves, our first fall back in the States. But now I absorb them even though it's winter. My fingers tap my wood desk. I rush to the piano in our dining room where I play red, gold, orange, bright.

At the next lesson I urge Mrs. K to listen. "Just listen."

"No," she says, after I play a few chords of the song. "We don't play by ear. We play what's in the book."

My fingers harden as if encased in ice. My feet in heavy loafers are rigid as if blood coagulates when they press pedals. How much easier to play barefoot, in the West Indies, my toes caressing metal, my fingers free, loose in tropical heat.

One day, down in the basement, I glance at my mother's easel. While the wintry scene could, *ideally*, convey sun-dazzled snowy trees, the light, instead, implodes on white paper. I glance through other paintings discarded on the floor. In one, autumn leaves are blocks of static color. And here is an image of me playing *this* piano. But the background—an ocean of wall-to-wall gold carpet in our living room—fades to the color of tarnished doubloons that a pirate lost deep beneath the sea.

What song did I rehearse for the spring recital? I no longer know. I only recall wearing a pink cotton dress with ruffles along sleeves and hem. I tie a pink ribbon around my ponytail. I sit before a polished baby grand on a stage in an auditorium filled with parents. I place my fingers on the keyboard. Halfway through the number my mind freezes. Stops. I can't remember any more notes. Not one. Every memorized chord evaporates. I stand abruptly and walk off the stage.

I never play again.

My mother insists I enroll in a typing class. After all, she earned a decent wage as a secretary, enough to help pay for her two brothers to attend college. She buys me my own manual typewriter, a Hermes, which comes in a cute green plastic case. I roll crisp white paper into the platen. I put one pinkie on the "A," the other on the quotation mark. My index finger, which once rested on middle "C" on the piano, now settles on the letter "F." Each finger is assigned its own letter, its own responsibility, within a neatly confined space. No need for imagination or fancy hand movements.

In class I type one practice exercise after another, mechanically following the textbook. After a few weeks my fingers, of their own accord, know where each key is located, much easier than memorizing notes. They like the sensation of pounding plastic letters. I even begin to hear a rhythm to the *tap, tap, tap*. I convince myself that this black-and-white clarity contains its own form of beauty. I type so quickly the keys jam. I enjoy separating them, allowing each to plop back into its allotted position. I feel relaxed typing—maybe even slightly drugged—as each finger automatically, without need to even think about it, reassuringly strikes the correct key.

I love the *qwertyness* of it all. I love the word "qwerty," formed by the letters aligned side-by-side on the top line of the typewriter keys, or just below the numbers. I think of myself as a professional Qwertyist. I imagine getting a reference in the *Merriam-Webster Dictionary* for coining this word to describe someone who learns a *practical* skill. Unlike a *pianist*.

One Christmas vacation, home from college, I visit my parents where they now live in an apartment in Weehawken, New Jersey. In these quarters, smaller than our suburban brick ranch, there's no room for my mother to set up her easel and paints. The upright piano has, however, made the trek, successfully hauled up three flights of stairs. The piano cover is closed. My mother has arranged knickknacks atop it.

To earn money over the holidays, I work in a bank in Manhattan. I spend eight hours a day in a cubicle, down in the basement, punching the keys of a clanking adding machine. Hour after hour scrolled paper, full of numbers, spews from the machine, numbers that must be meaningful to someone. The office is decorated with plastic garlands and silver-tinseled pine. The air smells of metal and money.

One day when I arrive home from work, my mother sits in the living room, her sewing basket on her lap. She wants to fix a hem on a dress. *Here.* She hands me the thread and needle. Even wearing glasses, she can't see well enough to slide the thread through the eye. I myself don't need glasses and easily fix it for her.

I sit beside my mother and pick up a tangled clump of mint-green yarn. A few years earlier, my mother taught me, or tried to teach me, to knit. Is she a believer in "idle hands are the devil's plaything"? Or is it the "devil's workshop"? Or is it "idle hands are the devil's tool"? Regardless.

I gaze at my mother's paintings hanging on the walls, all those images from a once-vivid island life. I see that young version of myself perched on the piano bench, fingers on keys. Even if I had continued to play, wouldn't all the notes have evaporated in the sheen of West Indian heat?

In this moment the loss of music feels deeper than sound.

Maybe I experience what Keats called "agonie ennuyeuse," tedious agony. A silence. A waiting. Waiting for, in my case, another form of music to arise. Waiting to discover the relationship between typing and language.

Just like my adored uncle did.

What did I learn from him as I sat on his wine-red carpet, or on his lap, illuminated and warm in the sun? I still hear the clack of typewriter keys on index cards, more persuasive than sounds of the city street below. Engrossed by the pressure of my own fingertip pressing keys, all else ebbed . . . as I created, I now believe, much more than solitary letters. The stack of index cards on his left was filled with black-typed words. The stack on the right remained blank awaiting its turn.

I wait for years, in silence, for my turn to no longer be blank.

But now, sitting beside my mother, I wonder: Who was that island girl back then—gone forever? Or living, forever, framed beneath glass? What was that Caribbean light, that sound and color, that paradisiacal, pre-Qwerty world?

MY DEATH IN THE FAMILY

essomenic: showing things as they will be in the future

I die at four years old.

My father and I sit on the wood floor in our house in Bethesda, Maryland. The radiant heat in the floorboards warms the backs of my legs. I wear corduroy slacks and a checked-flannel shirt. Even though it's winter, my father wears only a white T-shirt with his old workpants, unlike suits he wears to his important government job in the Truman Administration. Beside us is a stack of construction paper, scissors, crayons, and glue. He's building a toy for me, a paper house, with paper furniture, and a paper family. He uses dark red, the color of brick, for the outside walls. Inside, the walls of the kitchen and living room are white. The walls of my bedroom are pink, my older sister's blue. My parents' bedroom walls are—I don't remember—maybe the color of my mother sleeping, the pale gray of unconsciousness.

My father does most of the constructing while I watch. When it's time to form the mother, father, and two sisters, however, he sketches the outlines and shows me where to cut. I'm left-handed, the scissors are for a right-handed person, so I cut awkwardly, snipping off a crook of an elbow here, a toe of a foot there. The paper mother and sisters wear dresses. What does the paper father wear? Anything?

My father glues together a couch, a dining room table, dressers, and beds.

I place my paper father and mother in their bedroom, together in bed. I place the paper "me" in my room, alone in my bed.

Something is wrong.

The radiant heat from the floor feels too hot yet, simultaneously, too cold. I shiver, feverish, as if my body burns at the same time it solidifies into ice. I glance at my father to determine if he sees. Am I even still here? I pick up the scissors and press the blunt point against my palm. I feel it, but it's like a distant ache. As if it's both my palm and not. Maybe it's the palm of the paper girl.

I'm afraid of the paper girl. I don't know why. I pick her up from her paper bed and make a small rip, a tiny tear in her neck. My father doesn't notice. My father will never notice the small rips and tears in his nonpaper daughter's body.

He glues together a miniature refrigerator.

I know I must thank my father for spending several hours building a toy house just for me. I lean forward to hug him. He grabs me too close and kisses my lips. Quickly I look for my mother. She must be in her bedroom, sick. She's frequently sick, or thinks she is, suffering a litany of life-threatening diseases though she will live well into her eighties. My sister, in all weather, plays outside in the woods behind our house. When I look out the window, I'm never able to see her hidden behind trees. Or else she roller-skates through the neighborhood, her thin form wheeling around the corner, out of sight. She's rarely home. I should glue paper roller skates on her paper-doll feet, like tiny paper plates from which she could eat, when she's hiding.

Late that night my real father enters the bedroom of his real daughter. I pretend to sleep as he slides under the white cotton sheet and pink quilt comforter. He tugs up my flannel nightgown. His hands are too hot, too cold, as they stroke my legs, higher. Me. All of me. The fever I felt earlier returns. It's a fever that pulses through my blood stream, singeing my veins, my temperature exploding out the roof of my head. All this before the chill begins. Even the follicles of my hair shiver. My father pulls me closer to warm me. His fingers feel as if they are still sticky with glue, a kind of resin that adheres to my skin. I feel as if I'm suffocating. The scent of his bay rum aftershave is so strong all the real air in the room evaporates.

He dabs the bay rum on just for me . . . before he enters my bedroom.

No. No. Wait. I must be the paper-doll daughter.

I open my eyes. Even in the dim light I see the outline of the paper house atop my bureau. I expect to see flames roiling out windows, glass cracking, the shingles on the roof melting.

The paper people in the house are trapped inside just like the real people.

The next morning I'm by myself in bed. I tug down my nightgown and stand before the paper house. It looks undisturbed; there was no fire. I was so sure it burned overnight that I touch it to ensure it's still real.

The paper-doll girl looks as if she slept peacefully all night.

That's not true.

Standing on the floor in my bare feet staring at the paper house, I split in half. No, that's not true either. If I knew the word "soul" back then, I would say that, during the night, during many nights, my soul slips from my body evaporating to ether.

I retrieve the paper-doll girl from her paper bed. I'd forgotten to draw a nose, mouth, eyes, ears with the crayons. Her face is blank. Featureless. An effigy. A voodoo child. She can't see or taste or hear anything.

I feel as if I have died. I *have* died. I no longer believe I'm an alive little girl. Still, I feel the floor beneath my feet but, at the same time, I don't quite feel it either. Maybe I can be alive and dead at the same time. Maybe I have special powers. I can be present *and* absent in time and space.

Yet last night, or was it the night before, or will it be tonight, I feel as if my father cut open my spine, and everything labeled "me" tumbled out. I sit on the edge of the bed. I peek under the sheet. Nothing. Just a flat white sheet that smells of Clorox. No. It smells like bay rum, too. There is no scent of me.

This paper-like voodoo child is half-dead/half-alive. Her thin shoulder blades feel queasy. She's afraid to glance in the silver, gum-wrapper mirror. She might see only crayon features. Or, worse, no features at all.

In the doll's thin, vulnerable body, I see my own thin, vulnerable self. In order to survive, as a sort of test run, I must save that paper-doll me. Over time I draw one eye followed by another eye, a nose, a mouth, ears. I reinforce her neck with tape. I hide her in a glittery jewelry case where no one will find her. No one can touch her.

As much as I fill in the blank paper-doll features, I also, over the years, fill up pieces of blank paper—reinforcing those pages with words. Through the sheer force and power of words, sentence by sentence, I construct new facets of me. There's always another sentence, another facet to polish, which I hold in my palms, turning each to catch the light. As if that paper girl hidden in the jewelry box has herself become the jewels.

To survive death, I must first survive my father.

THE THREE FATES

Drawing the Shades

Imagine a house after a fire, one wall remaining. Imagine the scars leading to the second story where the staircase used to be. We are that scar. We are the tread of a footstep on a brick path. We are the underpinning of air. We are memories written across night in glow-in-the-dark paint. We are eyes the color of abandonment. We are lost toothbrushes of solitude, a graveyard of combs and orphaned socks. We are all the clichés and all the philosophies about the Meaning of Life and Death, but you won't learn about us from either.

We are not elusive. We are not omniscient. We are not a sweven, a vision, you might glimpse in a lunar halo. We are not piped-in music. You won't see our outlines reflected in a window or our shadows darken a mirror. We are, perhaps, a splinter in your eye.

We are merely the space between . . . when you know something is up.

A MEMBER OF THE WEDDING

vacivity: emptiness

On an otherwise pleasant summer evening in Michigan, I attend a wedding reception held on a driving range of a country club in Linden. I sit on a folding chair at table 22, a yellow napkin in my lap, beneath a giant tent decorated with twinkling lights. I'm acquainted only with the bride's father, busy overseeing the festivities. I know no one else. I don't feel like meeting anyone else. I'm not good at small talk under the best of circumstances and now, shortly after my second husband abandoned me, just the thought of indulging in "pleasantries" is exhausting. What would I say? Discussing divorce at a wedding is a buzzkill any way you slice it.

The band plays. Drinks flow. I partially listen to idle conversations.

On the back of the cardboard placard for table 22 is a photograph of the bride's dog. His face is dusted with snow. I later learn the photo is snapped through a window, the dog outside, looking into the living room. The dog's right eye appears eager: *The door will open soon. I will be in my warm home.* (Totally projecting human sensibilities onto an animal.) Yet the dog's left eye portrays such sadness I want to weep. I can't weep here in this tent with several hundred happy people.

The photo of the dog speaks to me—or maybe barks—especially the sad left eye. Often when I should feel happy I'm despondent, convinced tragedy waits to strike. Conversely I'm content, if not actually happy, in a crisis—knowing things can't get worse. So during the festivities I wear my psychic "do not disturb" sign. If this were a wake, I'd be right in my element. Table 22. Catch 22.

I hold the photo in my lap stroking the paper image. I want the real dog, in the fur, here with me now. I want to own the dog. I want to kidnap him, bring him inside from the cold. I slip the photo into my purse. The dog's name is Jersey, which maybe weights the moment with too much symbolism. But maybe not.

Years ago, for my own Jersey wedding, to my first husband, I purchase a sale dress costing $19.95 in a hippie boutique. I hedge my bets by investing as little as possible in this mistake that will last six years ($3.32 a year). The night before the wedding my face erupts in hives. I try to hide the red patches with makeup. But there I am the next day saying "I do," I guess, though I have absolutely no recollection of the ceremony. None. All I recall are the hives, the navy-blue dress sprinkled with velvety purple flowers, the neckline low enough for my former high school home economics teacher to have a stroke—had she been there. Which leaves the stroking-out role to my aunt who, horrified by the dress, never gives me a wedding present.

I don't remember saying "I do." But surely I wanted to say *I don't.*

I do remember this: I'm surrounded by wedding guests but feel as if I stare through a window trying to find a way into life. And if not *my* life, then anyone's. I'm not picky. Any life would do. In that moment, stepping into my husband's life, is the best, the only solution.

This man, my husband, is nice. But he is a stranger. We don't love each other enough. He doesn't buy me an engagement or wedding ring. I don't expect one.

Why do I marry him in the first place?

No one, before, has asked for my hand, let alone my entire being, in marriage. So maybe I'm grateful. One summer, when still in college, I worked in DC and lived at McLean Gardens, a residence hall for single women. I saw firsthand the future of a previous generation of solitary women holding teaspoons, every night at dinner, which they delicately dipped into glass goblets of rice pudding. It wasn't pretty. From blossoming to coffin, with no husband or family in between, was one slippery slope to be avoided. My marriage—to last *until death do us part*—takes care of everything. Doesn't it?

No. My second wedding occurs in the backyard of my run-down house in Texas. For this wedding I up the ante purchasing a mail-order dress for $39.95 and worth every penny. This marriage lasts twice as long as my first. A virtual eternity. Nevertheless, did my poor home economics teacher teach me anything? This two-piece, red cotton number with blue-and-white flowers is strapless and slutty.

During the ceremony all fifteen guests are attacked by a swarm of fire ants.

Am I unable to be a wife simply because I never learn to cook or sew? I never have children. I never learn things that seem more or less second nature to other women.

Initially, in high school, I (kind of) (more or less) (sort of) toy with becoming a woman who *will* cook and clean and sew for an eventual family. I even go so far as to take (because it's *required*) home economics from Miss Z. I purchase a few yards of dull-brown cotton material to craft into a skirt. I open the Butterick pattern, and I tumble into a crinkly wash of tissue paper tattooed with strange lines, notations, and designs. *The edge must lie on the fold, cut on the bias, to prevent raw edges and seam allowances from raveling, use zig-zag setting on the machine.*

But I myself am replete with raw, unraveling edges, no seam allowances whatsoever.

Nevertheless, I stitch together scraps of material that wouldn't fit the shape of any known body size on any planet in the universe. I snip the seams, pull out thread, begin again. Three times. Four times. I abandon the kick pleat. The hem sags, depleted. Grease from french fries smudges the front when I forget to wash my hands after lunch. The straight brown skirt with a kick pleat and one-inch waistband, envisioned in my head as well as in the pattern, fails, again and again, to materialize. It wouldn't even make a decent shroud.

In a revolutionary move, I hack five inches off the hem in order for it to feel freer, lighter. As if I wave a wand, I create a miniskirt even though the stitching resembles Frankenstein's monster's face.

The home economics class switches from sewing to cooking. My skills fail to improve. I somehow substitute sugar for flour in what is supposed to be a chocolate cake. I dump it into the trash along with the former hemline, hoping never to lower my sights or my hemlines again.

In English class that same year, still in a snit of causeless rebellion, I write a term paper about the Black Death, while other students research uplifting, inspiring aspects of history, such as the Renaissance, the discovery of gravity, the invention of penicillin, etc.

Even putting the bubonic plague aside for a moment, I know Miss Z's pre-Martha Stewart's vision of life doesn't exist. Never has. At least not for me. Nevertheless, does it seem contradictory if I say that I want(ed) it as much as I didn't/don't want it? But as much as I didn't want it, I do want it, but not enough to (have) pursue(d) it.

In short, I put all my diseased eggs in one casket. Maybe I flunked home economics on purpose. Maybe I flunked Home on purpose. Maybe I flunked Marriage (twice) on purpose. Thus, the eggs. Thus, the casket.

The photo of Jersey the pooch reminds me of my own childhood dog, a Scotch terrier.

A different Scottie lives two blocks from my house in Michigan. He lunges against his white picket fence whenever I pass his yard on my morning walk. He waits for me at the corner of the fence, waits, in order to race the length of it barking and growling until I'm out of sight. I could cross to the other side of the street. I could walk a different route. But soon I look forward to seeing him.

One morning I decide to bark back. We follow each other the length of the fence barking at each other. Do I think that if I speak his language he will acquiesce, accept me in his doggy universe?

One day as I approach his yard I don't see him until I reach the far end. There he is. Why hasn't he hurtled toward me? We contemplate each other, neither of us barking. Just as I'm about to step out of sight, he growls, half-hearted, just to let me know that he hasn't abandoned his essential dogginess.

He's inside his house on another morning. I see him through the window, his paws perched on the back of the couch. Smoke curls from the chimney. He gazes out at me. I want to sit beside him, close to him. He doesn't seem to be barking, but he follows my every step.

Once in seventh grade I hit my own Scottie with his leather leash.

This is the most immoral thing I've ever done.

Our family drives in the Plymouth, with my Scottie, from New Jersey to Londonderry, Vermont, for a Labor Day vacation. But before we leave the house, while packing the trunk, my father, in a rage that smells of zinc and rancid oil, yells at my mother, my sister, and me. We've packed too many suitcases. We aren't correctly placing them in the trunk. I want to put my case with dolls on top of the other suitcases, worried the dolls will be crushed. His toneless voice says I can't bring the dolls, period. I am ordered to return them to the house. He accuses my sister of bringing too many books. He yells at my mother because she forgot to pack snacks. The nails of my terrier click around all four of us, not pausing, as if trying to find the one member of the family to whom he most belongs.

My father's anger settles over our heads like sweat.

I clasp the handle of the case holding my dolls, unmoving. My feet are seemingly rooted to the floor of the garage. The cold from the concrete pulses up my legs to my kneecaps. I hold my breath as if that will diminish my senses. I will evaporate from this moment, this father, this house.

Driving along the New York State Thruway, my father yells about the traffic. He yells when I ask if we can stop for hamburgers. He yells when I say I have to pee, though he acquiesces when he stops for gas anyway.

My sister sits on the far right-hand side of the back seat, I on the far left. The air between us crisscrosses with edgy static. We ignore each other surely believing the other is the source of our father's fury—or as if we inherited a silent form of his fury. I don't know how to reach her any more than she knows how to reach me. Or maybe we look out opposite windows wishing for an interstate miracle. We will float free of the car, materializing in another car, adopted by another family. Another life.

Our Scottie walks back and forth across the back seat. He first stands on my lap to poke his head out my window, then my sister's. Maybe he searches for his own form of escape. Eventually he gives up and falls asleep between us.

Our father yells for 204 miles, his power a steady avalanche burdening his imperfect family.

I glance at the back of his neck hoping to see pustules—announcing the onset of Black Death—sprouting below the hair line.

We stay at an artists' colony located in a sprawling farmhouse. One afternoon I walk alone with our Scottie on a leash. The wide lawn spreads toward a field leading to woods. The terrier starts to bark. I stare at my dog as if I can will him to stop. He won't. I feel all the impotent rage of a girl who can't control anything, even a dog. Just below the sound of the harsh barking, I smell turpentine and fermentation, a chilly breeze on my face. Dead brush and leaves burn in the distance. Time seems disturbed, place fractured, as if I no longer know where I am or what I want.

On this day with too much wind and gusting trees it's as if the day itself is having a tantrum.

Then the snap of leather against the brindle fur of a Scotch terrier.

After I hit my dog, blood rinses through the veins in my left arm, cold and feverish, like distemper.

The dog stops barking. He growls.

The word "brindle" is from Old Norse: "piece of burning wood."
The autumn day contains the red scent of fire.
Is this what girls do when a father's love feels more like flame than warmth? Is this why the girl fails love?
Both the dog and I are burning.

November draws near, and the Scottie down the street in Michigan is out in the yard less and less. I don't see him for days. The air smells cool with abandonment. I feel separated from the world as if I stand behind a veil. I miss him, his tumbling energy defending his home, keeping strangers at bay, though now sometimes seeing me as "not stranger."

The first thing I do after this second husband leaves me, after his car pulls out of the driveway for the last time—love dying before actual death parts us—is purchase a fire extinguisher. Because I am now solely responsible for protecting a century-old house with questionable electrical wiring. I sit on the kitchen floor reading complicated directions on how to operate it. I'll never remember them. Should the house catch fire, only ashes will remain by the time I capture my cat Quizzle and figure out how to pull the trigger on the nozzle.
A fire extinguisher will not save me from certain death.
In short, I am alone in my house with Quizzle, a fire extinguisher, and (foreshadowing here) a Nazi flag in the basement belonging to my now ex-husband.
This is not Miss Z's or anyone's version of home, of life.
A solution: Perhaps that version contains homemade applesauce!
There is no way to explain how memory connects fire extinguishers to Nazi flags to applesauce, but the next thing I know I'm at the grocery store where I purchase a sack of Granny Smith apples. Back home, with no recipe, never having made applesauce, never even *considered* making it, I suddenly know how.

I peel the skins. I cut each apple into six wedges, digging out the cores. I drop sixty pieces of apple into a pan of boiling water. I stand by the stove, stirring, until the apples soften, more or less, to the consistency of sauce. I add about twenty teaspoons of cinnamon.

I wait while it and I simmer.

By ten at night, I fill a bowl with applesauce. I sit at the kitchen table and eat and eat and eat. Even before I finish one batch of applesauce, I cook up another pan of this improvised manna. Or can applesauce lead me to nirvana whereby I no longer need to worry about divorce, my house burning to the ground, or even death? Is this applesauce-nirvana Miss Z's version of a Perfect Life?

I fear I need more.

But because I don't have more, as the holidays near, I start lying. Compulsively.

I stand in line in the grocery store with bags of Granny Smith apples. I—who *never* speak to anyone in a checkout line, ever—hear myself saying that my two daughters, who live in New England, are coming home for the holidays! I've already bought the turkey/ham/sweet potatoes/pumpkins, but, oh my, I forgot apples for homemade pie!

The next trip to the grocery store I am the proud mother of two sons who live in California. I bring back my parents from the dead, my husband from divorce. *My in-laws are visiting, too,* I proudly announce. *A family reunion at my house. All the presents are bought. The tree is decorated. Oh, I wonder what my husband bought me for Christmas!*

On New Year's Eve after surviving, via prevarication, this first Christmas without my husband, I am alone with Quizzle. We sit before the television watching the festivities. Quizzle curls against my leg. I bought one present for myself, a package of six Godiva chocolate truffles. Beginning at 6:00 p.m. I will eat one chocolate an hour to lead me into 1998. I offer Quizzle one salmon-flavored cat treat an hour as well. I have brushed and combed her fur for our minor celebration.

Snow begins falling shortly before midnight. I don parka and boots and walk deserted streets in my quiet neighborhood. Christmas decorations cast green, red, gold lights across icy sidewalks and streets. Mine is the only dark house. In some homes parties are in full swing. In others televisions flicker. Where curtains are open, I catch glimpses of Christmas trees, fireplaces, knickknacks, pictures. Families. One year resurrecting itself into another.

I am the dog gazing in the window.

FATE 2 LACHESIS

measures the thread of life to determine how long you live

THE SICK HYPOCHONDRIAC

"Any disease that is treated as a mystery and acutely enough
feared will be felt to be morally, if not literally, contagious."

—Susan Sontag

cagastric: of diseases, originating under an ill star

At 11:00 p.m., here in my home in Michigan, I switch off the light. The
darkness isn't soothing. I'm wide awake. How can you guard against
death while sleeping? You have to be vigilant even when vigilance is
exhausting. Now I worry what's causing a mild headache. An allergy
to leaf mold? A sudden outbreak of lead poisoning? The longer I lie
awake, intransigently awake, disease after disease presents itself for
consideration as if I'm all the patients rolled into one on the TV show
House. Soon I'm convinced I've been nursing a small brain tumor for
years. Now it's metastasized into a lump the size of—what?—a peach
pit, an apple, a grapefruit? Tumors always mimic fruit. Hopefully with
a little luck—though I'm habitually an unlucky person—mine will
resemble a raisin. A currant.

I fetch my laptop, prop it on my stomach, and search WebMd.com.
The symptoms of a brain tumor include confusion and behavioral
changes. Well, the origin of my headache *confuses* me. As does the
throbbing. Yet I quickly develop rheumatoid arthritis either in addition
to or instead of the tumor, presenting as fatigue, which I feel, along
with insomnia and loss of appetite. Which could be true. But the

more I read the more likely it seems I suffer from fibromyalgia. These symptoms likewise present a problem with sleep.

Except when I turned on the computer my eyesight blurred: *multiple sclerosis*. Tingling, numbness. A few days ago when I awoke, all the fingers on my left hand tingled. But since I can't remember the exact date this occurred, I scroll over to Alzheimer's: confusion and behavioral changes. I throw in lupus for good measure, a disease option on virtually every episode of *House*. I get as far as "inflammation" before I think I might vomit, at which point I'm sure I'm developing a migraine or stroke.

Before I surf over to "migraine," a headline about "back pain" catches my eye. I've suffered low back pain since high school. *Don't always think back pain is back pain*, is the gist of the article. It can be a symptom of prostate cancer, abdominal problems, osteoporosis, Lyme disease, lupus (*I knew it!*), swollen joints, or bone cancer. Even though the back pain was alleviated by acupuncture who knows if it might reoccur as something else?

I click back to headaches and stumble upon an article about a woman who went to bed with a severe headache and woke up dead. Well, of course she didn't wake up dead since she *was* dead, but her husband found her lifeless body in the morning. An aneurysm blew out her brain. An aneurysm, a bulging blood vessel, is present in 5 percent of the population, all waiting to rupture.

Now I'm terrified to sleep because I might not wake up. I want to be awake when I die.

Wait! Didn't I just remember that I awoke a few days ago with all the fingers on my left hand tingling? I am a walking stroke!

Most strokes occur in the brain, so maybe the headache, which might be a migraine, which might be a tumor, which might be an aneurysm, is really a stroke. I have three hours before the brain blowout in which to take the clot-dissolving drug TPA, or Tissue Plasminogen Activator. In the United States someone strokes out every forty-five seconds. Bad odds. Bad, bad odds.

I can barely breathe. Heart attack? Stroke? Lung cancer? I click on heart attack and learn that pain on your right side might *also* be a sign. When the heart muscles don't get enough blood the damaged organ releases enzymes. *Go immediately to the* ER. *A simple blood test can check your enzyme levels.*

Who's to say it isn't any or all of these? I *should* go to the ER. At least I live only a few minutes away from North Ottawa Community Hospital here in Grand Haven.

A few months earlier, on a Thursday, I awoke in the middle of the night with abdominal pain. Trying, at this one moment in my life not to be a complete hypochondriac, I make the mistake of ignoring it. Over the next few days the pain ebbs and flows. I can't locate its exact position. It seems amorphous, free floating from the left side of my stomach to the right, from top to bottom. It *maybe* seems worse when I lie on my left side. So I figure I'll be fine, nothing further will develop, if I lie on my right side for the rest of my life.

Then I decide to worry.

Tuesday morning I see my nurse practitioner. She pokes and prods but no particular place hurts more than any other. She asks me to lift my right leg. I do. No pain. Not appendicitis. *Come back if it gets worse.*

It doesn't get worse; it doesn't get better. I see her again and am given a blood test for appendicitis. The blood levels return normal. *Go home and come back if it gets worse.*

It doesn't get worse; it doesn't get better. I return to the nurse who orders a CT scan for the following afternoon. *Don't eat anything the night before.*

The next morning the pain is virtually gone. I consider canceling the scan, but since I fasted all morning, I show up. They scan. I return home. The nurse calls two hours later: *Go to the* ER *immediately for surgery. Your appendix is inflamed. It could burst.*

I lie in the ER for hours waiting for the surgeon. I watch my stomach as if I'll be able to witness the explosion, the onset of poison peregrinating my bloodstream. I've never had an operation. But it'll be only laparoscopic, not too bad. Finally the surgeon arrives. He pats and pokes my stomach. No pain. He frowns. He pokes again. I kind of fake pain not wanting to be sent home again only to die in my sleep with a major rupture. Better to haul it out and be done with it once and for all.

I go home the next day minus an appendix.

But what's my body incubating tonight? Maybe it's an onset of swine flu caught from a person traveling from overseas. I have flown recently though I always wear a NIOSH N95 face mask approved by the World Health Organization and the Centers for Disease Control and Prevention. I also use MyClyns, the first antibacterial spray that can be sprayed into your ears, nose, and mouth. Its "non-toxic formula has been proven to kill 99.9% of viruses and bacteria, including E. coli and staph infections, is easy to use in planes or anywhere you come in contact with others." Like, say, *life*. I also never board an airplane without Flight Spray "to prevent viral infections by creating an unsuitable environment for inhaled germs to reproduce." To prevent Deep Vein Thrombosis (DVT), I wear "latex-free, Class 1 graduated compression socks to support and massage legs during long flights."

And I chug Umcka that "shortens duration and reduces severity of symptoms associated with the common cold and throat, nasal, bronchial irritations." Its medicinal and/or magical active ingredient is Pelargonium sidoides 1x (basically geraniums). I stockpile it and don't leave home without it.

Now a dark circle floats at the corner of my eye. I turn my head. It disappears. I stare straight ahead. It reappears like a gnat hovering in my peripheral vision. *Detached retinas.* "Shadows, flashes of light" some website informs me. *I see shadows.* The edge of my laptop, still propped on my stomach, casts a dark, blurry line on the bedspread. I immediately regret never learning Braille because I will need to know it by morning. I sweat. My stomach seizes. My headache worsens.

I check the top news stories on Yahoo while I consider whether to go to the ER. One headline states: "Girl Lucky to be Alive after Sting by Deadly Jellyfish." I feel as if *I* just escaped with my life though I haven't been anywhere near the ocean lately, to say nothing of Australia, where this occurred, given that Michigan is 807 miles from the Atlantic Ocean, 2,173 miles from the Pacific, and god knows how many miles from Australia.

"Girl Describes Swamp Ordeal." This horror story stars amoeba-naegleria fowleri, single-cell microscopic organisms that *eat your brain!* The article describes the death of a young girl whose brain was invaded after swimming in a warm, freshwater inland lake. One hundred and nineteen people have been infected with this organism since 1962; only one survived.

I remain awake the rest of the night.

Several months later, *that* headache cured with two Tylenol tablets, I awake with a tender spot on the left side of my stomach. I place my palm over it. Not a sharp stabbing pain. Not a dull ache. Sore and tender. A bruise under the skin.

Initially it feels like a phantom appendix haunting me. Perhaps a sliver of the original organ, left behind after surgery, migrated to a safer location on my left side. Maybe the rogue appendix, petulant over being uprooted, now *reroots* in order to regrow, metastasize. It's not taking any more chances of oblivion—who can blame it—and stages a coup on my torso.

That's what it feels like anyway.

Given my history of an *entire lifetime* of magical thinking about illness, disease, death, and other inconveniences, my brain zooms from rogue appendix to kidney failure to bladder cancer. I make an appointment with my doctor STAT.

As it turns out, when the hospital originally scanned my abdomen and discovered the inflamed appendix, a cyst was also noted on my kidney, my doctor *now* tells me. At the time it seemed benign. Maybe it's grown. Maybe a colony of cysts set up housekeeping in a neighborhood in the high-rent zip code of one desirable kidney.

I lie in a darkened room while a sonogram technician spreads a clear gel on my stomach, then glides a transducer across my abdomen. My insides are displayed on a screen—grainy black-and-white—throbbing and pulsing. The technician points out my abdominal aorta supplying blood from heart to legs. *An aorta in my stomach? Who knew?* I know virtually nothing about my body. Not my *actual* body. However, I know everything about my *metaphorical* body.

The technician maintains a running commentary, shattering my illusion that the body operates mystically either on good or bad juju. Though with the onset of this amorphous pain in my stomach maybe it's magic *and* science. The liver is the largest internal organ, secreting bile, the technician tells me. The spleen stores red corpuscles and platelets. The pancreas produces hormones, secretes enzymes. My bladder resembles shores of a lake, urine splashing like tides against the inner walls.

I want an organ specifically designed to monitor an existential crisis. An organ specifically designed to monitor loneliness and fear. An organ whose sole responsibility is to oversee *complete cellular regeneration!*

Yes, there is the cyst on my kidney, she points out. A dark solitary nodule hunkered down for the duration of my life. No colony sprouts beside it. The technician tells me that, as we age, most everyone develops cysts on their kidneys.

I visit my doctor who confirms nothing is amiss on the sonogram. He prods my stomach. He listens to it through his stethoscope. What language does it speak? Will it pinpoint its own pain through echolocation? Apparently my doctor hears nothing revelatory. "Maybe you pulled a muscle," he suggests. Given my sedentary life, I can't fathom this diagnosis. He sends me on my way.

My doctor, though nice, always seems rushed when he enters the examination room: Hurry up, give me the facts. The suite of medical offices is a warren of exam rooms containing one infected or diseased body per cubicle. The doctor lurches from contagion to catastrophe dispensing, I imagine, bad news, leaving a trail of despair behind him. Or he dispenses pharmaceuticals that leave a trail of life-threatening side effects, and profits for the companies, in their wake. Or, finding nothing obvious, there is neither diagnosis nor cure.

I temporarily abandon Western medicine and see my acupuncturist, Stephen Durell, at West Michigan Acupuncture. Stephen, unlike my doctor, approaches me smiling, relaxed, unhurried. Patiently he listens as my disjointed, untuned-to-my-body mind, tries to sort out the nuances of pain. He's optimistic he can help, which, in and of itself, is a relief. Not that acupuncture cures everything. But it eases the journey for some ailments while curing others. When I had a bulging disc in my spine, for example, I was approximately two minutes away from surgery when the magic of acupuncture saved the day. No surgery. No negative side effects.

Now, acupuncture will lessen this current pain, whether it's caused by a pulled muscle or something else. Stephen inserts thread-thin needles into my stomach, legs, hands, and scalp. They open previously blocked portals allowing fresh blood to be released and rerouted. Positive energy flows through me realigning my body's meridians. I lie on a bed, lights dimmed. New Age music shimmers. I inhale lavender, lemon, cloves. Pain ebbs. Calm reigns.

I also try Reiki: a laying on of hands. It's not a biblical myth. For an hour the palms of the Reiki specialist whisper over my frame. Warm energy seeps into me.

I trust needles for my meridians and palms for my chakras.

For extra protection I use Thieves Essential Oil Blend Lozenges.

Legend has it that five thieves looted homes of victims of the Black Death, sometimes even strangling those not yet dead. They also stole money from corpses in the street. As if possessed of supernatural powers, these thieves never contracted the plague themselves. Caught looting in Toulouse around 1628, they were given a choice: *reveal your secret and be hanged; or don't reveal it and be burned at the stake.* They chose the less painful death. They admitted to being descended from a long ancestry of perfumers who discovered the curative powers in certain plant oil extracts. According to French aromatherapy doctor Jean Valnet, the recipe used by the thieves included white wine vinegar, wormwood, meadowsweet, juniper berries, wild marjoram, sage, cloves, elecampane root, angelica, rosemary, horehound, and camphor.[1]

My tin of Thieves lozenges contains xylitol, sorbitol, citrus sinensis, clove buds, lemon rind, cinnamon bark, eucalyptus, rosemary, and peppermint. A new recipe for new plagues.

What I *really* want is not to be composed of matter at all. I want to be reborn increately, or re-created without a body. And soon. Because in the span of a few years this very un-increately body seems determined to liquidate itself with the speed of a going-out-of-business sale.

For example, from an unfit doctor who prescribes Clindamycin—an antibiotic that should be used *only* when all else fails, like for something as serious as the *plague*—I get a c-difficile infection. It disrupts the good flora in my intestinal track. I lose about twenty pounds in a month before a gastroenterologist diagnoses the problem and provides a cure. Now, because my body is overly sensitized to antibiotics, I get *another* c-difficile infection after the appendectomy.

Following these medical emergencies, I discover a scabby lump on the right side of my nose. Tiny. Only a little larger than the point of a pencil. A pimple? Insect bite? But it's not red. In the mirror I eye it suspiciously. I turn my neck to view it from different angles.

"A tumor," I say to Marc, my partner.

"It's not a tumor." He sighs. He's been living with me and my tumors and humors, my vapors, maladies, ailments, and malaises, for over ten years now. Only a few manifested into a full-blown illness.

One evening a few days later, washing my face, the small scabby thing falls off. A spot of blood. Then nothing. "My tumor is gone," I say to Marc.

It reappears two days later. I make an appointment with the dermatologist. "It might be nothing," he says. "Or it might be basal cell."

"I prefer the 'nothing' option," I say.

The biopsy, however, confirms basal cell. "But if you have to get cancer, it's the best kind," the dermatologist says. "It doesn't enter the system. It doesn't kill you. But it still has to be removed." With the scrape-and-burn procedure, cancer cells, distinct from healthy skin, flake off easily. I envision a substance such as friable asbestos.

The basal cells are expunged in under ten minutes. A muddy hole darkens the side of my nose. A Band-Aid is slapped across the mess. *Call if you see signs of increasing redness, swelling, heat, increased pain, or yellow drainage.*

So here I am driving home from the dermatologist's office in my nifty cowgirl hat with turquoise beads—remember?—alone inside my body. Well, my soul sits inside my body squashed among various organs. If only I could house my soul elsewhere. *One soul, please, hold the body*—thus entirely bypassing fragile-on-the-cusp-of-self-destructing-any-minuteness.

Currently I have a persistent cough the cause of which my doctor is unable to pinpoint.

So of course I'm a sick hypochondriac! Who wouldn't be? Each body part is subject to numerous and multiple diseases. I don't know how it's possible to survive even an hour without full-onslaught tragedy.

Maybe life would be easier if I believed in god or any religious form of Life after Death be it heaven, hell, purgatory, limbo, or some waystation in a distant planetary system. But I don't. There will be no godlike *deus ex machina* to swoop from the sky in the final seconds to save my ailing body. My fears are corporeal, not spiritual.

I survive by obsessing, by numerous consultations with Google, M.D. What else to do with an obsession other than pick it clean? I'm a scavenger of obsessions refusing to part with any, especially one fertile as death. At least as long as it still has a hint of life. And death still has plenty of meat on the bone. My ability to worry is the one aspect of me that will never grow old.

It's like an addiction, a need, as I drag my body time after time to a doctor, a specialist, a hospital, a clinic, a lab where they draw blood and X-ray my insides. I want tangible proof my body exists twenty-four hours a day.

I also survive by attempts to metaphor my way out of each disease or potential source of death. Or if I print the name of a disease on a piece of paper I, in effect, open it up, letter by letter, to unscientifically understand it. Or, better yet, excise it altogether. Not being a medical doctor, it's all I have left. It's my only recourse. The body speaks an arcane language. I must learn to translate.

To survive death you have to believe in the magic of language.

I do.

THE THREE FATES

On Tedium

The same, every day. No visitors. No afternoon tea. The polished peacock-colored cups remain unused. This constant dusting, hoping one day . . .

But who are we, after all, to complain?

Hours—so many hours to walk the streets to spy inside windows. Noticing the slight hitch of a curtain. A baby's wail. Is it time? Is it time?

Our arms are linked but we never touch.

We digress.

When we pass strangers, we want to take a pulse. But how quickly dim faces flee. And then we return to empty teacups. No stains rim the lips.

THE SAFE SIDE

*palmoscopy: observation of heartbeat or
pulse as part of a medical diagnosis*

The triage nurse asks about my symptoms as I huddle at the ER registration desk in Grand Haven. They know me well by now. Last night, I tell her, I felt pressure against my heart. And sweating. I don't tell her I feel fine now. Nor, this morning, do I even consider an appointment with my primary care physician. Test results as an out-patient take days. I want answers. I want them *now*. In the ER you get instant gratification even if the news is bad: *two weeks to live*. If last night's episode was a heart attack, it's apparently not life-threatening. Yet I swoon over the reception desk to *appear* frailer than I feel. This claim must seem legitimate.

The word "heart" bumps me to the head of the line. The wide doors to the treatment rooms swing open.

I change into a hospital gown, slide onto the bed, and describe the symptoms to a nurse. She checks blood pressure, pulse, temperature. All normal. In fact my blood pressure is low. She attaches electrodes over my upper body for an electrocardiogram. Cold, gooey patches dot my skin. She explains this shows the electrical activity of my heart. Impulses, recorded as waves, flow along a monitor *if* you're lucky. "The muscle of an injured heart *doesn't* show electrical impulses," she says. I press a finger to my chest. A gentle thrumming. I'm not flat-lining. Yet. But the overly processed air in the ER, the discordant noises, the flashing and beeping, the unrelenting fluorescent lights, don't sound like the real world. I almost feel as if I died last night—halfway between awake and asleep—or not knowing the difference. And if it isn't a heart attack, how to interpret the mystifying message sent to me by my heart?

Last night I *think* a flutter in my heart awakens me around midnight. From the start, however, I'm confused by my lack of conviction or empirical evidence. Perhaps I haven't yet fallen asleep. Perhaps I'm in a state of semiconsciousness.

Whether awake or not this is what I feel unless I hallucinated the entire episode. No, let me make one definitive statement. This *is* what happens: My skin sweats, mildly. A thin pressure encapsulates my heart. The pressure deepens, but softly, as if a palm cradles it. Then, for a brief moment, the hand hugs it. This mental image is distinct. No arm is attached to the hand, only a portion of a nondescript wrist. Is the gesture meant to convey a farewell? A greeting? Love? A subtle warning? In this quasi-conscious state I'm not scared. I passively accept this gesture, whether it's a vision, a dream, or something else.

Then I fall asleep.

In the morning I remember the sensation. Now, more alert, I want to understand. It felt good, but was it actually bad? A heart attack? Perhaps a metaphor. If so, for what?

Another nurse, carrying a slotted tray of test tubes, pulls back the curtain encircling my bed. She's here to draw blood. "What'll that show?" I ask. Apparently, if the heart has been damaged, certain enzymes leak from it into your blood stream. I imagine chartreuse-colored enzymes contaminating my veins because the word "enzyme" *sounds* chartreuse. I might be dying, so indulge me. She slides a needle into the crook of my elbow and fills vial after vial of blood.

Next up is a chest X-ray. I worry about radiation but, at this point, I'm too far into the heart attack scenario to say "never mind." They maneuver my entire bed out the door, the aide soundlessly gliding me down one linoleum corridor and up the next. A breeze gusts my skin. I experience the sensation of floating through space. Who knows where I'll land?

I'm still here on earth, however. The technician asks me to stand in front of the machine. "Don't move. Hold your breath." When I ask what the X-ray might reveal, he replies, "fluid in your lungs. Also, the size of the heart and the blood vessels." *But won't the X-ray appear skeletal*, I wonder, a vest of ribs protecting a defenseless heart. I want to ask the technician for a copy of the X-ray, a snapshot to be saved for a photo album. Not that I believe in ghosts or otherworldly creatures, but what if a hand has been dispatched to my heart with a message? I want to see it. I want to know the message.

I'm wheeled back to my room, a double, which now contains another patient. A man coughs and sneezes, spewing galaxies of germs into the air.

I nod my head toward the man and ask the nurse for a face mask, the kind surgeons use to protect themselves from the common cold, Ebola, the plague. She sighs but gives me one. The man seems closer to death than I. The nurse must understand how hard I work, on a daily basis, keeping it away. Why isn't everyone as vigilant as I?

The ER doctor sits on a stool and scoots close to me. He wants to know my symptoms, what happened last night, what did I feel? I again explain the sweat, the pressure on my heart. He waits for me to say more.

"It was gentle," I say, hoping he can hear me through the face mask. "Friendly."

He puts down his pen. He flips through my chart that might, at this point, contain the results of the blood and X-ray tests. He looks at me. "I've never heard anyone describe a heart attack as *gentle*," he says. "Or friendly."

"Maybe it was a *little* heart attack," I say.

"I'm scheduling a stress test for you," he says. "Just to be on the safe side."

"Now?" I ask.

"Three days," he says. "But the ECG, the blood work, the X-ray, all are normal." He is not unfriendly, exactly, but suspicious. "Sometimes, you know, people imagine things," he adds. "Especially when they're stressed."

I want to tell him *of course I'm stressed*: about *dying*. After all I've been stressed, or so it seems, about dying since birth if not before. Isn't he himself terrified by the sheer *nothingness* of it all? I also want to ask him if it could have been symbolic. Isn't it just as important to unravel the meaning of a symbol or a sign as it is to diagnose a physical symptom? Isn't there a test for that?

Three days later I report to the Nuclear Medicine Department for the stress test, which will determine if I had a heart attack or not. I want to declare that I am suffering the aftereffects of a metaphor and call off the test. But being a hypochondriac, I can't.

So here I am, trapped in a high-tech-fluorescent-lit-nuclear-medicine chamber.

A myocardial stress test determines whether blood flow to the heart was blocked long enough to have caused damage. I sit on a chair while the nurse ties a thick rubber band around my upper arm. She plunges a needle into a vein injecting me with radiopharmaceutical Tc99m Myoview. It takes time for the material to flood my system, though I expect to glow electric-green immediately. With a cheery smile from the nurse, I'm encouraged to go to the cafeteria for breakfast. *Return in an hour.*

I order an English muffin and a bottle of water. I sit alone at a small round table. A few doctors and nurses, at neighboring tables, laugh and eat. I remove a pencil from my bag and, on a paper napkin, I write: *For breakfast I had an English muffin with a radioactive chaser.* Not exactly a balanced diet. *Surely I did not have a heart attack. The radiation will kill me instead.* It reads like a suicide note. No need for an autopsy. If it weren't for the radiation coursing through my system—if I didn't feel like a nuclear bomb about to detonate—I'd sneak out and go home.

I'm given a cardiac computerized tomography before the stress test. I lie on a table inside a doughnut-shaped machine while a tube rotates around my body collecting images of my heart and chest. I turn one way. Then another. The machine whirrs. I want a copy of this procedure as well. I want to see inside my skin. Who am I? What was that gentleness? What was that shadow? What do I look like on the inside? Can such a printout convey—if not the actual distance or length of time between me, today, and my eventual but hope-to-be-avoided death—a history of my life? What I really want to ask the nurse is whether these machines and tests are smart enough to differentiate between heart attack and metaphor.

I'm next brought into a room with a treadmill as if this is a gym, and I'm here for a workout. If this is a test, I'm sure I'll flunk. While I walk half an hour every day, let me emphasize the word "walk," as in "saunter." I've been on treadmills only once or twice, and they seem intimidating.

The machine starts slowly. No problem. Piece of cake. The nurse turns up the speed. I don't even break a sweat. My heart doesn't feel as if it's about to attack. They speed it up and, again, no problem keeping pace. I feel as if I'm accomplishing something significant as making it through the Olympic trials. The doctor studying a printout smiles. The nurses beam. They crank the machine faster. Surely I'm soaring back and forth in time as if the computer will spew out a complete history of my heart from the moment I was born to now. I'll understand everything I need to about my heart and soul—if I have one.

Finally the machine slows before stopping. The doctor tells me I have the heart rate of someone at least fifteen years younger.

How then to explain that hand holding my heart? I didn't dream it. What was it? Whose was it? What did it mean? Was it a warning? A message?

Sometimes people imagine things, the doctor said.

But death is my obsession, I should have answered. I imagine *everything*, every possible kind of death! Little everyday deaths. Near-deaths.

Death-defying deaths. Emotional deaths. Existential and metaphysical deaths. Minor inconvenient deaths. Pseudo deaths. Final death. I need a system that ranks various deaths on a scale from zero to eternity.

After I return home, I Google symptoms for a "gentle, friendly heart attack," which the doctors don't think I had in any event. I find sites that describe a squeezing pain in the center of your chest, pain in your shoulder and arm, even your teeth and jaw. Prolonged pain in the upper abdomen, shortness of breath, sweating, fainting, nausea, clammy skin, fatigue. Besides the sweating, which could be symptomatic of anxiety and stress, none of these descriptions fit me. Nothing about shadows or symbols.

I must discover what it is.

What other words pertain to the body to make it more of what it is—or more *than* what it is—keeping me on the safe side.

The side of life.

MY LIFE AS A THANATOLOGIST

somandric: pertaining to the human body

"You have an E. coli infection in your bladder," my doctor says over the phone, after receiving the lab report. He prescribes Macrobid. Two tablets a day. Seven days.

I sink onto the top step of stairs in my house in Grand Haven. As good a place as any to die. I consider tossing myself down the steps but that would only result in quadriplegia. I prefer dying of a bladder infection, allowing E. coli to spread to my kidneys—and organ-ic points beyond—rather than swallow the antibiotic to cure it.

I glance out the small window across from where I sit. Winter sun glazes the pane transparent white. *My soul hovers outside the window.* I close my eyes. Silence whispers against my lashes: like ash, like smoke. I press my forehead to my knees.

Infections = antibiotics. Antibiotics = death.

Because of those two c-difficile infections caused by antibiotics, I'm now at risk for another whenever I take almost any antibiotic. The only hope to avoid a reoccurrence is to take the one "good" antibiotic, Vancomycin, designed to combat c-difficile, in conjunction with the "bad" ones that cause it.

It's a battle between Good and Evil—Life and Death—of epic proportions.

It might work. It might not. Additionally I take Florastor, a pro-biotic designed to prevent c-difficile. It might work. It might not.

My mind spinning, I slam into my car and drive the five minutes to my doctor's office. I don't know why. He has already handed down my sentence. His medical practice, attached to the hospital, probably has a morgue. Rather than take the elevator to the second floor, to Internal Medicine, I should press "B" for basement, an obvious location for a morgue. Better yet, an "M" option should be available on the elevator panel. *Go directly to the morgue; skip the preliminaries.* I should check in as if it's a motel. Forgo the turning-the-body-inside-out steps to keep the body alive once c-difficile rampages through organs, muscles, tissue, sinews.

I will not relate the embarrassing meltdown in my doctor's waiting room. I refuse to describe my sobs at the receptionist's counter. I refuse to mention how I grab off my glasses with such force they break. I am out-of-control pure plasma sloshing around inside my skin. I repeat, repeat, repeat, repeat, repeat, repeat: *I must see Dr. A immediately.* I must see him because then I will decipher a secret meaning in his message. The message will withdraw the E. coli from my system. It will prove the diagnosis a mistake. It will commute the death sentence.

"He doesn't have any openings this afternoon."

I sit in the lobby anyway. Waiting.

Across the room a woman huddles on a chair, her winter cap pulled low over her forehead. A man in shirtsleeves, as if it's summer, stares at the ceiling. I want to throw myself at their mercy and beg for them to give me their appointments. I assume my emergency is more important than theirs. Can I bribe them? I stare at the same spot on the ceiling as the man as if it's a sign.

I search for evidence of things unseen: E. coli, my bladder. My soul. Maybe I don't have E. coli. I want proof. I can't see a swallowed antibiotic careening through my system. My interior world is invisible, only logical in its own illogical state of (non) being. In the past when I had those c-difficile infections, my body emptied itself. I felt weightless.

This incident is happening now on February 13, 2015. Today, a week after I collapsed in my doctor's waiting room, I finish the seven-day supply of Macrobid. For seven additional days, four times a day, I'll continue with Vancomycin. 5:00 p.m., 11:00 p.m., 5:00 a.m., 11:00 a.m. Then I wait . . . I will wait for one week, two weeks, a typical amount of time during which the c-difficile infection might still invade and trample my system. Right now I don't know what will happen.

And because this is *ongoing*, as I write this, how to select the voice to best present this episode? If I know I won't get the infection, I'll be ironic. I'll step outside the moment and observe it from a slight distance. A historical self, a self that knows the outcome, will filter the drama calmly, more insightfully.

If I get ill, however, irony is the wrong tone. Death, or near-death, deserves nothing less than full-blown melodrama. Like a lurid red-and-orange sunset in a bad velvet painting. Like a clown with lipstick smeared across his face. Like strands of garlic, Stars of David, and crucifixes dangling from the ceiling, strung around my bed. Like I'm levitating, my body limp and vibrating.

Words defining death sound harsh, cold as marble, definitive, final: "gravestone," "ashes," "plot," "inter," "exhume," "mausoleum," "casket," "formaldehyde," "bury," "cremation," "fossilizing," "crypt."

Vault: A burial chamber, especially when underground.

But "vault" has positive connotations, too: a room for safekeeping documents, jewelry, anything precious. If all the words describing life are protected, will they be safe for eternity? If I lock myself in a vault will death lose track of me?

As a child I played in the vault in my father's bank in St. Thomas, the West Indies Bank and Trust Company. That Danish colonial building had thick stucco walls built to withstand hurricanes and pirate attacks. The vault had an impenetrable round steel door. Entering it was like being swallowed by a sea creature, as if I had wandered into distant realms of Ultima Thule—yet not scary—rather, hidden and shadowy. I sat on the floor inhaling moist limestone, parchment paper, a coppery scent of history. Vaulted away in luxurious solitude, I felt safe in case a long-banished pirate materialized from a distant century.

Years later, in the 1980s, I lived in Galveston, where I worked with my first husband who directed a historical preservation project. The organization's headquarters was housed in a Victorian building, originally a bank. A small room, once a vault, was my office. Even though its steel door was removed, I felt sheltered entering its arched passageway. The inside walls were covered in a substance similar to aluminum foil—I have no idea why. All day as I worked, I glimpsed vague shadows, flashes of light, distorted yet oddly comforting images of myself. I wanted to live there, take up permanent residence, protected from disaster, disease, contamination. Death would never see me, would most certainly bypass this hidden enclosure. If The Fates came lurking, I would be camouflaged as a thin beam of light.

A vault seems a perfect place to be locked away from time and mortality.

Or, sadly, *if* captured by Death, I could still live there but in a different, much reduced, bodily form.

Over the centuries, places of burial have varied since, to date (*only* to date), no one has yet to survive death. In the Middle Ages, in London, the dead were buried, literally, in walls and vaults of the church. It was considered a "distinguished form of interment." But interment was first used during the Neolithic period (4000–2500 BC) and "consisted of long barrows. These were vast walk-in burial chambers covered by mounds of earth." By the Bronze Age, cremation was mainly used; "bodies were burned in pits, and the cremated remains buried in collared urns beneath smaller, rounded burial mounds."[1]

In medieval times people were buried in pits. When one pit was filled, it was covered in earth and "a previous one reopened. The bones were dug up and taken to the charnel house for safekeeping. The term derives from the French *charnier*: flesh. In France and Italy, skeletal remains were used to create artistic displays, including chandeliers, which were exhibited in the ossuary—a gallery above a charnel house."[2]

Maybe, if worse comes to worse, I can be reincarnated as a chandelier, always burning bright. Better yet, I could add my bones to the approximately 40,000–70,000 skeletons decorating the 1870 Sedlec Ossuary in the Czech Republic. Also known as the Bone Church, it, too, has a "splendid chandelier composed of almost every bone in a human body. The ossuary displays two large bone chalices, four baroque bone candelabras, six enormous bone pyramids, two bone monstrances, and skull candle holders." There is also a chain of bones hung like "crepe paper at a birthday party."[3]

A few years ago, drafting my will, my attorney asked if I wanted to be cremated or buried in a cemetery. The word "cemetery" is from Greek *koimeterion* or "dormitory." I don't want to live into eternity lined up with other skeletons. Nor do I want to be reduced to rubble. For starters, I'm offended by the boring unoriginality of these options, given the fact that death, *if* it comes, is a once-in-a-lifetime, superextraordinary, over-the-moon event, to which no one, nonetheless, is lining up for tickets. If, however, I must list something in my Last Will and Testament and assuming, for example, that the Czech ossuary is no longer accepting donations, my next choice is to be mummified and interred in a pyramid.

In 2011 Alan Billis, a British taxi driver who died from lung cancer, became the first person to be mummified in 3,000 years. Dr. Stephen Buckley of York University conducted the procedure based on decades of research, which actually improved upon ancient Egyptian techniques. "Buckley first coated the body in pine resin, beeswax and sesame oil, before lowering Billis into a natron salt bath. Left to dry in the water bath for a month, Billis was subsequently wrapped in linen bandages coated in oils, resins and spices." Speaking prior to his death, Billis said he supposed his legacy would be that of a pharaoh.[4]

And in several thousand years he'll probably resemble one from the 18th Dynasty.

I wonder how much real estate remains available in the Valley of the Kings. Pine resin, beeswax, sesame oil: readily available substances. In my bathroom is an antique, claw-foot bathtub. I could fill it with natron salt in preparation.

Or I could replicate Jeremy Bentham's disposition of his body. In the late 1700s he requested that his skeleton "be put together in such a manner as that the whole figure may be seated in a chair usually occupied by me when living. . . . I direct that the skeleton be clad in one of the suits of black occasionally worn by me. The body so clothed, together with the chair . . . will be prepared in an appropriate box or case and will cause to be engraved in conspicuous characters on a plate to be affixed . . . on the glass cases in which the preparations of the soft parts of my body shall be contained."[5]

A fallback position, Plan C, is a lifelong pass at Window of the World Amusement Park in Shenzen, China, which features a ride whereby people, packed into a coffin situated on a track, enter a faux morgue. As the ride commences, you roll into a brick structure resembling a giant fireplace or furnace. Once inside, machines, set at 40 degrees Celsius, blast hot air at your body. Afterwards, "volunteers see a womb projected on the ceiling and must crawl until they reach a large, white padded area . . . where they are 'reborn.'"[6]

An even *better* option, and closer to home, is *Pharoh's Fury*. Shaped like a funerary boat, it un-furiously sways back and forth on the midway, a featured carnival ride during Grand Haven's Coast Guard Festival. I imagine floating down the Nile before suddenly veering into the Grand River. I'll sail across Lake Michigan in an ancient papyrus funeral barge that transmogrifies into a ship of pure unadulterated Egyptian plastic. The ship's prow swells into the shape of an enormous pharaoh's head.

A sign by the ticket booth, on the midway, states: "You have to be this tall to ride." It should say "this *dead* to ride." But don't pharaohs live forever, albeit mummified, in pyramids?

At night the plastic jewels on *Pharoh's Fury* flash red, green, gold like a neon promise. This *could* be ancient Egypt or at least a real-enough facsimile. *Me* . . . sailing in a jeweled boat toward the Afterlife. The perfect compromise between life and death. Neither life *nor* death— neither underground burial nor cremation—and much more elegant than "surviving" as a display of bones. My body, encased in faux gold, shimmers in an indestructible plastic ship floating down the Grand River.

In short, I'm resurrected for an all-expense-paid vacation on a *Pharoh's Fury* cruise to the Afterlife. I'll star forever in a reproduction of my life with the Sun God rising over a frozen field of Michigan blueberries. Me, sailing, sailing—ropes of pearls around my neck, turquoise eyes, a garnet heart—outdistancing the Curse of the Pharaohs, the Desires of the Furies, the Inevitability of the Fates.

Or, another promising option: I'll return as Miss Route 17, back in the gold Plymouth, gripping not the *Book of the Dead* but *Book of the Forever Un-Dead*.

Rilke writes, "In those days people knew (or suspected) that they had death inside them like the stone inside a fruit."

Maybe the best medical procedure is to remove the stone at birth, leaving the fruit intact.

Still I wait for a c-difficile infection.

After I left the doctor's waiting room that afternoon, followed by days lying in bed assuming catastrophe, on February 22, at 10:23 p.m., I snap. My body feels encased in a blister containing bacteria, viruses, death. I'm convinced the bladder infection has returned, which would mean another regimen of antibiotics. At the same time, I'm convinced c-difficile rampages through my intestinal track. I drive immediately to the emergency room.

I know the drill. I enumerate the existing and/or possible nonexistent symptoms. Hospital gown. Bed. Blood pressure. Pulse. Temperature.

A nurse draws blood. Vial after vial fills with mysterious red liquid. Another nurse asks whether I smoke, drink alcohol, what's my marital status, race, religion. I want to ask if there's a box labeled "vampire." Who wouldn't want to feed on such warm, luscious nectar?

Another nurse inserts an IV for fluids, though what's the point of nutrition if I'm dying?

The ER doctor pulls back the curtain. He's the same one who treated me for the non-symptomatic faux heart attack, who kindly suggested the attack might have occurred in my mind, not my heart. He stares as if he might recognize me, but I don't flinch or remind him of our past relationship. He shuffles through the papers handing me the results of my tests. I expect the worst. He provides the best.

As much as there is a language for dying, there is also a vocabulary that covers every molecule of blood and urine.

Blood: White blood count, red blood count, hemoglobin, hematocrit, corpuscular volume, platelet count, segmented neutrophils, lymphocytes, monocytes, anion gap, glucose level. All normal.

Urine: protein, glucose, bilirubin, nitrite, leukocyte esterase, specific gravity, epithelial cells, hyaline casts, granular casts, amorphous crystals, bacteria. All normal.

"I know *you* think the bladder infection returned," the doctor says, "and that you have c-difficile, but no tests show this."

"Well, that's good," I say, relieved, stunned. I believe him; I don't believe him. I want to say that I'm *okay for now* at 11:57 p.m. But I'm convinced if they run the tests again after midnight the results will reveal a different story altogether.

"Sometimes, when we're scared, we *think* maybe we're sick, but . . ." He shrugs.

Hospital sounds fade. I no longer hear the doctor probably still telling me it's all in my mind. But maybe it's in my DNA. Maybe I inherited hypochondria from my mother. My mother's sister died from cancer, young. Subsequently, my mother "contracted" every single form of cancer that lasted an hour, a day, a month—until she miraculously recovered—or a new cancer staged a coup superseding the previous one.

Again I glance at the test results. *Amorphous crystals.* I don't know what it means. I don't want to know what it means, at least literally. Un-literally, amorphous crystals sound like a necklace, jewelry to ward off disease and infection. Maybe my various body parts, if not the whole thing, can be reincarnated into a jewelry display.

Or . . .

Even if I die, I want my DNA always safe and sound just waiting for a hint of moisture, a drop of dew, a vial of blood to bloom back into being, those double helixes spiraling into eternity.

Eternity at Tiffany's. Except I will not, of course, go lightly.

THE JANET LEIGH VARIATIONS

aceldama: site or scene of violence or bloodshed

For example: "Aceldamas, especially for women, are all around us whether we see and recognize them or not."

In 1898 John Roll McLean, a wealthy businessman who owned the *Washington Post*, commissioned John Russell Pope to design a grand Georgian Revival summer home in D C. Later, an 18-hole golf course, cast-iron swimming pool, tennis courts, stables, Italian gardens, and fountains were added, along with an iron fence surrounding the complex. After McLean died, his son, Edward, inherited it. However, Edward and his wife blew through their inheritance on one thing or another, including the pear-shaped "Star of the East" diamond and the supposedly cursed Hope Diamond. In 1942 the federal government bought the property to build housing for defense workers during World War II. After the war the Hartford Insurance Company bought it to be used as rental property.[1]

Which is where I enter the picture, albeit a few decades later. . . .

. . . when McLean Gardens, as it's now called, is transformed into a women's residence complex. I rent a room here one summer between college semesters while working as a Capitol Hill intern. It's located at 3600 Wisconsin Avenue, but if you drive by today (circa 2015), the entrance is on Porter Street, where you'll see elegant condominiums. In short, it has gone upscale since *my* summer when tastefully shabby rooms are rented to people holding on to one of the bottom rungs of the rickety limited-opportunities-for-women ladder.

After work I exit the bus and enter the complex through the iron gate—keeping all us single women in—and the unpredictable world out. My tiny first-floor room contains one twin bed and a dresser with an attached miniature bathroom. It smells like the 1950s, redolent of talcum, solitude, and scented hankies. No men allowed inside the rooms. Ever.

I wash city grit from my face. Then I stroll along the sidewalk to the cafeteria, passing trimmed lawns edged with delicate flowers. I'm one of the few women (well, girls) in a miniskirt and love beads. I eat fried chicken, potato salad, and apple pie with chocolate ice cream. The cafeteria reminds me of Howard Johnson's, my favorite place to eat: Formica counters, waitresses in aqua uniforms, and jaunty white caps of perfection.

That summer I meet Clark, the grandson of the senator for whom I work. After flirting for about ten days, he returns as planned to his home state of Alaska. We correspond, his letters arriving in my small mailbox. I'm drawn to the distance of the relationship, the cleanliness of emotion expressed on paper—no wrinkled, damp sheets. I enjoy the longing more than I would have enjoyed the consummation. I happily read the letters before refolding them, sliding them back in their neat envelopes. I sit in my room and write *Dear Clark*, filling sheets of paper awash in the slow, safe vibrations of McLean Gardens.

Years earlier, the night I see *Psycho*, my family and I, on vacation, stay in a guesthouse in New England across the street from a cemetery. (I wouldn't dare make this up.) *That* night, of all nights, my parents opt for an out-of-the-way-off-the-beaten-track place. They say it will be a more *interesting* experience for my sister and me. Never mind that I *hate* interesting experiences in terms of lodging. I long for the spick-and-span-ness of my beloved Howard Johnson's, where no mother-fucker with a knife as big as a sledgehammer will suddenly plunge through a white shower curtain, *stabbing, stabbing,* as black-gray blood swirls down the drain of a black-and-white movie. Which, you pray, will never be a biopic of your own life.

Ironically, that first time I see *Psycho*, I don't get it. I'm too young to understand the Freudian overtones: that Tony Perkins's character, Norman Bates, subsumes or is subsumed by his mother, etc. It isn't until I see it again years later that I realize mother and son are one and the same, and we should all be on the lookout for psychotic breaks. Beware lonely alienated men obsessed with their mothers who live in the middle of nowhere, who need therapy, to say the least or, better, a life. So they won't take *your* life prematurely.

But back then the point of the movie to me, the takeaway message, is that you don't (do *not*) venture off the beaten track when it comes to lodging.

That night in the guesthouse across from the cemetery, however, nothing happens. At least nothing happens outside of my overactive imagination. *In* my imagination, I wait. I'm on high-alert lookout for Janet Leigh to pull up in her car, fleeing, but driving straight toward that demented gleam in Tony Perkins's glassy irises, lighting the way to her doom.

The phone rings one evening in my room in McLean Gardens. My mother, crying, says that my Aunt Sylvia, my father's sister, was raped and murdered.

I prop open the door to my room. Even though muggy summer drenches the evening, I think the air will cool me, will help me breathe.

My aunt is, or was, married, with three daughters. She lives, or lived, in a beautiful house in the Chicago suburbs, where she owns, or owned, her own successful antiques shop.

I imagine her in her store, that late afternoon. I see her dusting Victorian chairs and Tiffany lamps after her last customer leaves. She hums to herself, pleased by how much merchandise she sold. She counts the money in the cash register and fills out the bank deposit slip. She thinks about what to fix for dinner for her husband and three daughters.

Does she first, simply, sense the man, like a suffocating breath on the nape of her neck? When does she glance at the rear door where goods are delivered? Does she hear that door whisper open? Surely she smiles at the man since she knows him. He is one of the men who delivers antiques to her shop.

But her smile fades when she remembers no delivery is expected today . . . when she sees him unbuckling his belt . . . when she notices the knife in his hand.

Later that summer, asleep in my first-floor room, I awake to *snip, snip* by my window (which, trust me, is still a better sound than *slash, slash*). My eyes open. I stare up at a gray-white ceiling. My sheet is kicked to the foot of the bed. A sheen of sweat covers my skin in this un-air-conditioned room. Do I hear his breath just outside the screen, his body pressed against bushes, his heavy soles planted in dirt?

Do I turn on the light? Do I call out? Do I scream?

As strange as it seems now, *I don't remember.* All I know is that nothing further happens.

In the morning I stand outside my room with a security guard staring at the cut section of screen.

"Could it be someone you know?" the guard asks. "Someone you met, even casually?"

The night before, I danced and drank a few underage screwdrivers at the Tomfoolery. I met a man. From Germany. My mother, who came of age during World War II, who experienced antisemitism firsthand in America, always warned me to stay away from Germans, which, of course, I ignored. He escorted me home. *I don't even remember his name.* I mean, I never *heard* his name correctly in the first place since it sounded, well, German.

I shake my head at the guard. "No," I say. "There's no one."

That summer I am too young to see the women of McLean Gardens as anything other than widows, spinsters, aunties. Secretaries hoping for a husband and children, a comfortable home in the suburbs, or at least a promotion. Or as grannies patting dry lips with white napkins after finishing rice pudding, a dessert that leaves no one with gastrointestinal distress.

I am too inexperienced to see that the single women of McLean Gardens know something I don't. They understand how much the odds are weighted against them. Against us. In exchange for safety they are willing to accept an isolation that sometimes bleeds into loneliness, which is not as good as solitude, but better than being lonely alone. After all, John Roll McLean originally named his palatial estate "Friendship."

I wish for these women to be variations of Janet Leigh. Women who take what they deserve but, unlike Janet Leigh, get away with it. Women who stash the stolen money in the trunk of the car, hit the highway, but do not die.

After the security guard uselessly examines the cut window screen, I return to my room. I close the door, this heavy, humid Sunday. I lie on top of the bedspread. I stare at blank walls, almost white, almost gray. Traffic drones just beyond the gates. The sludgy afternoon stagnates. I hate Sundays. I've always hated them. For believers, Christians, it's a day to meditate, to give praise, to consider the promise of eternal life in heaven. But I'm neither Christian nor a believer. For me, Sunday is not a day that makes me consider salvation or love, but a day that turns my thoughts towards things like the darkness under boardwalks.

Immobilized, I remain on my bed. I hum *Eleanor Rigby*, a song recently released. It's such a perfect song for this place that I wonder what lonely people hummed before it existed. For that matter, where did lonely women live before McLean Gardens existed? Where will the women go once the property becomes gentrified?

I don't stay much longer. If I had, that Sunday-and-Eleanor Rigby loneliness might have become chronic, might have come after me with its knives. But only lyrical, metaphorical ones. Better to be attacked by *those* than by real knives—always dangerously nearby.

THE SUMMER OF
HATE AND DEATH

commendaces: funeral orations; prayers for the dead

For example: "I want to whisper commendaces for the dead.
But why aren't chants available *before* someone dies?"

April 1968, at 9:25 p.m., the first window shatters in DC.

My college boyfriend and I are dancing at the Tomfoolery on Pennsylvania Avenue when we hear the news. We want to *see* the news, live, in living color. We leave the bar and drive to the outskirts of Fourteenth Street to Seventh, H Street to U, two white kids in a Volkswagen Beetle out to watch race riots.

A crowd rips the iron grille off a liquor store, attacks shoe stores, mom-and-pop groceries, cafes. We cruise downtown streets into the asphalt heat of the city, ash flaking our windshield.

This is not Route 17. Flames aren't flashing neon. This is not the rage of a few juvenile delinquents ripping off the local drugstore for a pack of cigarettes on a boring Saturday night.

It's not so much that we aren't safe here—though we *aren't*. But sightseeing a race riot means we're simply stupid white kids with nothing to offer, nothing helpful to do. Useless.

That night, I don't know shit.

I don't even *know* I don't know shit.

Later that week, I break police curfew to walk the few blocks to my boyfriend's apartment. A man sidles next to me. I act cool but walk faster. *He* walks faster. His clothes smell of cigarettes. He holds one and asks for a match. *I don't smoke*, I say. He says maybe he's Jesus Christ. I want to say you should *know*, one way or the other, before making the commitment.

In the distance, sirens.

The man seems more homeless and lonely than dangerous, but who's to say?

I reach my boyfriend's apartment and rush to the front door.

The man who might be Jesus curses.

My boyfriend and I leave his place at 2:00 a.m. We cross the street to his Volkswagen, so he can drive me home. Jesus has departed. I walk around to the passenger side as my boyfriend opens the door to the driver's side.

I don't see them approach.

It feels sudden.

One man has a hand on my shoulder while another man points a pistol toward the head of my boyfriend. *Your money*, they say. *Give us your money*. I throw my purse at the man. My boyfriend pulls out his wallet. The man grabs the watch from my boyfriend's wrist. I hear a dull click. A second dull click. The men run up the street, quickly running away. My boyfriend tells me the sound was that of the gun jamming. A misfire that misses saves his life, my life.

Around the same moment as this incident—though I won't hear about it for months—my friend Joanne is murdered in New York City.

I imagine it: sometimes too quickly to capture details, sometimes in slow motion. Joanne in bed with a man. Frayed bedsheets. Dirty jeans. A tattered sweatshirt. Drug paraphernalia. A bulb sways from the ceiling, shadows distorting walls, for I see the murder only in *film noir* black and white. No knock on the midnight door. Wood panels kicked in. One man? Two? Guns. A bullet meant for her drug-dealer boyfriend, but there she is, a woman, always the wrong place, always the wrong time.

Her father later tells me that he heard about the murder while watching the late-TV news in his living room in Tom's River, New Jersey. No names released pending notification of family. But he knew, he tells me. Immediately he knew it was his daughter.

I hadn't seen Joanne in years. As kids, we sprawled in her bedroom reading movie magazines, waiting to be discovered. We stared at our ordinary faces in the mirror on her vanity table. We applied eye shadow, mascara, lipstick, as if we sat in a makeup trailer on a Hollywood set. She wanted to escape the muggy saltiness of Tom's River. She was sure one day she'd be on TV.

Now, right now this minute, I can't even remember her last name.

Yet I forever see her in that bed in an apartment that smells of scorched electrical wiring, peeling paint, and drug residue. I see her as the bullet homes in.

I'm unable to fully mourn her death. I never cry.

I hold death at a distance. Because once you invite death close to you, you—or I—will become a scrap of paper in an all-consuming flame, a wisp in someone's memory, someone who almost remembers your last name.

HERE BE HUMAN DRAGONS

redamancy: act of loving in return

One Friday a couple of years into my first loveless marriage, I run away for the weekend with a man who drives a blue convertible. He's an orthopedic surgeon moonlighting at a hospital in Beaumont. We drive over the causeway leaving behind Galveston Island, where I live, leaving behind his wife and my husband.

The doctor-on-duty is given a private room in the ER to rest between medical crises. He stashes me here while he works. I lie on the hospital bed staring at nothing. The song "Islands in the Stream," a duet between Dolly Parton and Kenny Rogers, which played on the radio driving here, continues to play inside my head. *Sail away with me.* I want nothing more than to sail away with the man in the blue convertible, driving the car out into the Gulf, across the sea.

That evening, while convertible-man fixes broken limbs, I go to the movies. I sit inside the dark auditorium while "Islands in the Stream" still loops around in my mind. I am an island in a *dry* stream. I know that convertible-man is on the cusp of leaving me after a two-month affair. I am merely waiting to be abandoned on a shore littered with bones. Silence envelops me until I can't hear the movie. I slide down in the seat. I close my eyes. The scent of popcorn and sugar makes the back of my throat metallic and hot, blistering enough to evaporate an ocean of saliva. *Love is blind. . . .* Nonlove is not blind. I see that the doctor will leave. But I can't see how I arrived here with him in the first place—a man who doesn't love me—anymore than I convinced myself that I love him. Flickers of light from the movie screen flash against my lids, strobing my mind, interrupting what I want: a smooth life instead of haphazard events and thoughts.

Later I again lie on the bed in the hospital listening to my mind repeat, repeat *sail away with me*. The man in the blue convertible will *never* sail away with me. I know I'll never see him again once this weekend ends. He will return to his wife. I will return to my husband who, working all weekend, will barely notice my absence. There is no one with whom I might sail away from this inevitable narrative.

Or wait: I *will* sail away but alone. No one else can go where I venture. No one can stop this trip. I will sail out the open roof of the man's convertible as he speeds back across the causeway Sunday night. I will land in an ocean of bones.

It's not yet Sunday night.

Even so I accurately predict the future. I already see, before me, that ocean. Not a salty ocean scent but medicinal—plaster casts, harsh astringent—how the doctor's hands smell when he enters this hospital room where I wait for him between emergencies.

Or as if *I* am the emergency.

An unseen emergency. You don't yet see the jangled intersection between the man under the boardwalk and this man. Here. Now. You don't yet see the many moments locked together with a lost key.

No windows interrupt the hospital room. No flowers. Medical supplies and equipment line the walls. One is an EKG machine to determine whether the patient has a heartbeat. I press my palm to my heart. Still here. Still there.

I wear a white-canvas sailor jacket bought at an Army-Navy Surplus store in Galveston. He unbuttons it. He slides down my khaki shorts and underwear. *I have my period*, I whisper. He shrugs. We're on a hospital bed—sheets, a mattress—accustomed to absorbing blood.

He will fuck me. There is no other word for what we do. "Islands in the Stream" repeats, repeats, repeats.

He must have drunk a glass of water. When he kisses me droplets from his mustache dot my upper lip.

We open our eyes, stare at each other, when we do what we do to each other. His eyes are pale blue. Gray? So pale they seem rinsed by sleet. I can't imagine what or who he sees when he observes me in these fluorescent lights. Why don't we switch them off? Switch our eyes off?

He is paged to return to the ER. He pulls on his scrubs.

I remain naked on the bed in a hospital room that's white, bleached, antiseptic, acidic, except for a splatter of blood. The only trace of me. This is what crime scene detectives examine after a murder to determine who killed the girl, how, and why.

For years after that weekend in the emergency room, I hear "Islands in the Stream" rasping my skull. Sure, it's an easy-listening kind of song, pure melodramatic country-western, love tilting, inevitably, toward heartbreak. When I hear it, I envision plaster casts, broken limbs, a splatter of blood, an ocean of bones.

Maybe that weekend I sit on a shoreline waiting for a Gulf of Mexico sun to scorch the skin off *my* bones.

I torture myself with memories. I prefer bad memories to good ones. I prefer to remember pain more than pleasure. I carry such memories with me as if in a knapsack, a weight I'm unwilling to relinquish. Pain is more mysterious. It will take several lifetimes to comprehend it.

Death terrifies me. Yet I constantly live or recall miniature forms of it: heartbreak and pain sung to a country-western beat.

It's six in the morning, Sunday, and I walk alone to the hospital cafeteria. The blue-convertible man is setting the bones of two drunk teenage boys who were in a wreck. Their blood must be splattered all over their car. The hospital intercom pages doctors. The corridors hum with the skim of rubber-soled shoes hurrying from one disaster to another.

In the cafeteria I order eggs over easy, toast, orange juice. I stare at the plate of food but can't eat. I rest my chin on my palm. I stick the tines of the fork in the egg yolks. Yellow spits across a bone-white plate. The back of my throat tastes like mercurochrome.

Here I am still in my body, *a* body, with all its complicated maintenance to stay afloat—food, sleep, water, shampooing, cleansing, vitamin D-3—the body and its slovenly, cumbersome, time-consuming need to survive.

Does it need love more than sex?

But, really, isn't its only true job that of being a container, a receptacle, to hold a soul? I want a better prototype. One less needy. One that better solves the problem of housing souls, lost or otherwise.

One that knows the difference between dragons and men.

One that knows how to live.

Not just exist.

Live.

MISS ROUTE 17'S
NEAR-DEATH EXPERIENCE
UNDER THE BOARDWALK AT
THE NEW JERSEY SHORE

Unforfend: unable to avert or prevent something evil

I am a smudge on the map of the Jersey shore.

I am no longer a smudge on a map.

I am here.

It's still that Friday afternoon in high school when I drive the Plymouth from north to south Jersey, down shore, and pull into the driveway of my family's summer cottage. Remember? In my white Keds sneakers, I walk the boardwalk to the carnival awash in the taste of Fralinger's saltwater taffy, peanut brittle, cotton candy. I sit on a wood bench on the boardwalk overlooking the ocean. Yes, *that* beach. *That* bench.

I've delayed this moment as long as possible. Yet the memory is always with me. Like that feeling when awaiting dusk. A lingering insufficient amount of air before the frenzy of night.

There I am.

Here I am.

I walk down the warped steps and along the wrack. I scuff through seaweed. To my left is the darkness below the boardwalk, deep as unconsciousness, fragile as shells splintered across the sky. To my right waves curl, foaming the shore, a wedge of moonbeam, enticing as sorrow.

Left? Right?

I stand in an ecotone, a transition between safety and danger. Between silence and sound. Beside an ocean that exhales and forgets to breathe.

The knife-thin man, with flint-cold eyes, steps from beneath the boardwalk and grabs my shoulder. He smells of wild pine barrens, of acidic lust.

Left: The choice is no longer mine.

Left: Feet stumble, dizzy and upended, the girl's body consisting of disjointed parts.

Left: Danger pulses like carnival lights reflecting a knife, reflecting my skin, electric with fear.

Left: Darkness foams whitecaps drowning my eyes shut.

Left: I am wet as ink that never dries . . . smudged hieroglyphics across a blankness of white paper and sand.

Left: His hand pins my long braid as if staking it into eternity.

Left: My heels make small indentations as he pushes my legs apart.

Left: Unzips my soul.

The Ferris wheel spins, unearthly.

A wisp of a soul levitates from a somatic body.

A few weeks later, after the knife-thin man under the boardwalk, I feel—or see—miscarried blood smudge the pink-tiled bathroom in my family's seemingly pristine house in Glen Rock.

I clean up the blood in the bathroom. I do not turn on the light.

I tug at the knob on the medicine chest. I grasp a bottle of aspirin. The label is red. Is it red? I empty white pills from the red vial into my palm. I turn on the faucet. I put each pill, singly, onto my tongue. I scoop water into my mouth. Pill by pill, I swallow.

I stare at myself in the mirror. Rather than see myself more clearly, my image hardens. I am a girl trapped in glass. Unmoving. Almost featureless.

I sleep.

I imagine myself tumbling inside the atmosphere of time, into the soul of time, drifting in airlessness. Weightless.

I wake up. I don't know how many hours later.

I wander out of my bedroom into the living room, a room with wall-to-wall gold carpeting. The texture feels cold, cold as metal, under my bare feet. No one is moving. Is anyone home? My Scotch terrier wanders in from the kitchen and presses his damp nose against my ankle. His brindle fur is sculpted in small curls along his spine. He returns to the kitchen. His nails click linoleum. He crunches food.

No cars pass outside on the street. No scent of hydrangeas. No shouts from neighborhood kids. No jingle of bicycle bells. Sun scorches the front lawn. The asphalt on the street appears soft. If I ventured out and stepped off the curb I would sink in tar.

I avoid glancing inside the bathroom. I don't want to see what I might see.

Instead I return to my bedroom. I feel heavy as if I'm shuffling within another body—that I am two bodies—so not quite me. The sheets are still warm. My head's indentation remains on the pillow.

The painted eyes of a papier-mâché dragon mask, which my father brought me from Thailand, perched atop my bookcase, stare at me unblinking, uncomprehending.

Is it my brain or is it a memory that sloshes in numbing ice water?

The venetian blinds are closed. Slats of a vitelline-yellow sun ladder the floor. I lack the strength to climb it.

SIGILISMS OF MISS ROUTE 17'S
MANY HIDDEN TALENTS

sigilism: act of revealing the secrets of the confessional

aischrolatreia: worship of filth, dirt, smut

CONFESSION #1: THE BEGINNING OF THE AFFAIR

You recline, drowsy, on the *terraço* of the Quinta da Capela in Sintra, Portugal, writing an aerogram. The thin paper is supported by Graham Greene's *The End of the Affair*. Across the valley rises the Palace of Monserrate and, beyond that, the Praia de Adraga, currents flowing from the Gulf of Cádiz, azure and hot. Beside the lounge is an oval table with a silver pitcher of spring water. Slices of lemon, round as miniature suns, circle a silver tray. You place a slice in a crystal goblet, fill it with water, and sip.

On this two-week vacation, you are with your husband and your friend, Dan, who owns this seventeenth-century stucco villa.

You are writing the aerogram to a man in Galveston, where your husband and you live. You're writing to that doctor who drives a blue convertible with whom you will have an affair.

Yesterday, your husband, Dan and you visited a cathedral. You no longer remember its name or which saint it honors. Afterward, Dan took you both to a restaurant for lunch where, outside the large windows, an angry mob demonstrated against . . .

You paid no attention.

In the aerogram you do not describe sightseeing excursions or local politics.

You write about silver pitchers, lemons, the blue Iberian breeze.

Your skin smells of Feno soap: moss, pine needles, the underside of a cork-oak leaf. The man to whom you address the letter will, one day, smell it.

From the valley rises the warm, spicy scent of eucalyptus and heather, lupine and poppy. Cerise bougainvillea etch whitewashed walls. You drift in sun, in shade from cork-oak trees, sun and shade, pages of the book, the aerogram, fluttering against your palms.

The day is transparent. You see straight through it watching time itself alchemize the globes of lemons, the sweetness of spring water, into images freighted with memory and presentiments.

CONFESSION #2: THE BLUE DRUNK

After you return to Galveston from Portugal—still unhappy and unhappily married—you attend a black-tie party with your husband. It is a business reception with people important to his career. You glide around the ballroom of a restored Victorian mansion, now a house museum. Your silky, slinky blue dress swirls your ankles, your matching satin high-heel shoes. You weave among groups of wealthy patrons who hopefully will write checks to assist the restoration of historic buildings. You briefly join a conversation here, another there. Everyone knows you, but you don't feel known. You're an indecipherable Rorschach. For no one knows that you're unhappy and unhappily married, awaiting the right moment to bolt.

You pluck Veuve Clicquot from the bar, continuing to flit around the ballroom. You drink the champagne straight from the bottle. The fizz sizzles your throat. You're drinking too fast but can't stop. You spill a bit onto the toe of your shoe. You laugh. You watch your husband deep in conversation with a man, both perfectly attired in tuxedos. Your husband doesn't even glance at you. Would it take a more indelible stain for him to notice?

Another man, a doctor, *that* doctor, notices. He taps your bare shoulder.

Without pausing to see if anyone watches—his wife, your husband—you and he, blended together, glide into the night in his blue Chevy convertible, top down. You cruise along the seawall toward the South Jetty. He parks on hard-packed sand. This is still weeks before you and he drive to that emergency room in Beaumont, the weekend you hear "Islands in the Stream," in your head, by the hour. In short, this is at the beginning of the affair not the end, when you still believe in bright futures.

You and he step from the car. Now you hear the song "Galveston," if only in your imagination. You kick off your blue satin shoes. He holds a bottle of Mateus rosé. Again you drink from the bottle. The moon appears slashed in half, a jagged beam wedging the water, a murky path out to sea. The sand is cool, damp. You scuff your bare soles as you walk beside him, half dancing, carving evidence in the beach. In the breeze off the Gulf, the hem of your dress swirls, brushing the skin of sand. Why not fast-forward to heartbreak and skip the preliminaries?

Instead he takes your hand. You keep pace with the music, walking in time to waves roiling the water. You return to the car and lean back on the still-warm hood. In that moment you feel love. In memory you see the blue of his car dark as your dress, as the night, and all you inhale is *blue, blue, blue.*

CONFESSION #3: THE BACHELOR PARTY

You should have learned your lesson but didn't.

One humid evening you find yourself, with otherwise respectable married women like you, driving drunk down Seawall Boulevard in Galveston. Dressed as prostitutes. Reeking of champagne. Careening toward a bachelor party.

Earlier, at the bachelorette party, you all ransacked the bride-to-be's closet searching for clothes with an attitude. The result is a faux-Hollywood-fantasy-meets-middle-class-women-in-their-20s-meet-the-Three Stooges. You wear short-shorts, a skimpy lace top, stilettos a size too large. Polka-dot knee socks. Scarlet lip gloss. Mascara.

You resemble a little girl playing dress-up.

You are *not*, however, a girl playing dress-up. Back then, when it's still funny to drink and drive, you are a slurring-words wife behind the wheel of the bride's Lincoln Continental. Invincible. Positive you're driving the speed limit. Positive you're in the proper lane propelling straight between the lines . . . a graduate, after all, of the Route 17 School of Driving.

You park down the street from the bachelor party. The bride decides you should all surreptitiously enter through the rear patio sliders. Sneak up on the guys: *Surprise!* After several bottles of champagne, you all believe this is a good idea. To you it's a *particularly* good idea since your own husband, who would ordinarily be at the party, is safely out of town on business.

You bruise your knee climbing over the stucco fence. You half fall, half jump, onto the soggy grass below, the stilettos nailing you to the ground. As you yank the heels loose, mud daubs your hands. You don't have a tissue, so you wipe them on the back of your shorts. You all stagger into the kitchen where the bride hauls another bottle from her bag. The cork pops. Foam fizzes. You all pass it around before heading toward the den filled with the sound of disco music and blurry voices . . .

. . . where you hear the fake moaning and panting of *real* prostitutes, stripping.

Undaunted and so obviously dressed for success, you hoist yourself onto the pool table. In front of the prostitutes, in front of your husband's friends, *your* friends, you dance. You sway as if in a spotlight, lashes lowered, slowly unbuttoning the flimsy top. You're not sure how far you'll go with the striptease—you've undone only about three buttons—when someone yells: *she's got a gun!*

One of the prostitutes points a pistol, successively, at each of your girlfriends—and you—because you're all mocking them.

Does the story of your divorce start here? Or is this the *death* which *do us part*, part? Homicide, after all, would be less humiliating and disgraceful than divorce. Worse, you fear this scandal proves that your husband shouldn't have married someone who could think this evening was a good idea. Which you do. Or at least did.

The men converge on the woman with the gun. They grab it, grab her, grab the other prostitutes, all while shoving money at them. The men hustle them out the door.

You lower yourself until you sit on the edge of the pool table.

You lower yourself until you slide onto the floor, onto the wall-to-wall shag carpeting. You lower yourself until you can't slide any lower.

Until you do.

CONFESSION #4: SUICIDE ATTEMPT

After the bachelor party, I return alone to my apartment, six zip codes past sober. I sit on the floor in the bathroom beside the toilet. The lid is down even though nausea pounds the roots of my hair and the backs of my knees. I close my eyes. For the first time I most clearly see the smudge of miscarried blood on the pink-tiled floor of the bathroom In New Jersey. I still see now, years later, the girl, that teenage girl I was back then stumbling, alone, from beneath the boardwalk, still stumbling, a few weeks later, down a short corridor from her bedroom to the bathroom with black wallpaper decorated with pink-and-white flowers, pink tile.

Her stomach cramps.

The teenage girl in New Jersey bends over the toilet thinking she needs to throw up, but her throat is empty. Dry. Vacuous. Hollow.

That girl feels lighter than sky. Eviscerated from her body.

The cramp deepens.

The girl slides onto the toilet seat. She bends over, her forehead on her knees. She wants to believe rose petals are sprouting from between her legs, drifting from her body.

But.

She smells tarnished scalpels. Dark. Mineral and metallic. She feels curdled blood dripping down her thighs.

The night empties. The soles of her feet press the floor. Sweat drips down the back of her neck. Her hair tumbles on either side of her cheeks. Her knees squeeze together as if she can prevent blood that is more than blood flowing from her womb. That girl has not once—not ever—thought the word "womb." It's not a word she wants to adhere to her.

It no longer adheres to her.

That night in New Jersey, in the past, the girl feels a form: amorphous, silent, lipless, lidless, boneless, armless, throatless, earless, lifeless slide into the water in the toilet. This form that lacks form is nothing more than a vaporous promise. The girl wants to look. She doesn't want to see. She feels as if blood seeps down her hair, her neck, her legs, her ankles.

The girl reaches for this liquid, tissuey form, tries to grasp it . . . hold *her*. But that form is pure liquid. Atoms shredding. There is nothing to hold onto. Nothing.

She worries the blood will never stop. She feels waterlogged with loss.

I, who I am now, still feel waterlogged with loss.

That teenage girl wanted, *wants* to hold that formless form all night. *Her.* But there was nothing to love, nothing to hold.

Now, in Galveston, I open the medicine cabinet just as I had that night in New Jersey. I remove a vial of Valium. I tap pills into my palm one by one. I don't count.

I am unable to prevent the pattern from repeating.

Again.

Again.

I am still seventeen. I am twenty-eight. There is no difference between seventeen and twenty-eight.

There is only this present tense.

Again I turn on the faucet.

Pill by pill.

Again I put each pill, singly, into my mouth. After each one I scoop water into my palm, into my mouth.

Pill by pill I swallow.

Again I stare at myself in the mirror. An image immobilized in glass. Unmoving. Frozen. Featureless. A frozen white light, a searchlight, unmoving and unforgiving.

The inside of my body drifts like snow.

I sleep.

I slip once again into a watery eternity smudged as ink. Fearing death yet drawn to it over and over . . . death bruising my eyelids into a staticky sleep.

I wake up. Is it the next morning after that bachelor party? Or have I slept through two mornings? My senses vibrate. My forehead tingles. My arms smell like darkness and zinc. I feel the bricks of the building pressed against cement. A viscous sun stains the sky. An airplane rips the clouds. The floor beneath my knees is colder than winter. My ribs crunch when I breathe. All my hair seems to shed. My heart is in a syncope state of beats unraveling.

Later that day I wander the island, neighborhoods of unrestored Victorian, Carpenter Gothic, Italianate houses. I meander The Strand, abandoned iron-front buildings, awaiting rejuvenation. Suspended. Soon, in a year, maybe two, stucco will be painted. Brickwork will be water-blasted, each individual brick repointed. Wood will be scraped and painted in bright Victorian colors until Galveston once again resembles the Wall Street of the Southwest.

For now, though, the island's adrift. Overgrown palmettos, oleanders, crape myrtles swoon in heat. On heavy humid afternoons the Gulf Coast sleeps. Saltwater stains ancient mahogany. Wrought-iron fences rust until Galveston itself seems scented with verdigris.

During its heyday would young women wearing proper Victori-an clothes have wandered here? Or would all well-bred nineteenth-century girls be home safe with parents or a husband?

Time feels porous. That staid century seems almost present, but I can't enter dressed incorrectly, as I am now, in a white tank top, a pair of cut-off jeans, and leather sandals.

Has time passed? Maybe this is limbo.

Maybe the historic buildings will remain as wreckage. Maybe the upcoming restoration project is more about preserving decay.

At dusk I walk to the beach. I wait, on the sand, only inches from water . . . a liminal space, a liminal moment. Day sinks into the Gulf. The moon disappears from the sky. Before me is a distant, unknowable haze of air and water. Behind me stand buildings pregnant with ruin.

DEATH COMES FOR THE POET

coxcomb: a vain and conceited man, dandy

fizgig: a flirtatious woman

See, way it happened, he died. Sudden. Single. Okay, divorced two, three times. Youngish. Or at least before his time. In the City. Uptown near Broadway, case you're looking for fingerprints. Or a body. No one in attendance when it happened, far as you know. Unless some married dame snuck from his apartment undetected. Though the way you *wish* it had happened: a gal with the same homicidal fantasy (no way else to say it) as you.

And who would say he didn't deserve it? You say he did, and you have your reasons.

But your hands are clean. It's the late 1990s by then, and you haven't seen him, oh, since the late '80s.

Just the facts in obits, police reports: Alone. Heart attack. Case closed.

Night. A three-alarm emergency strobes out his heart like Times Square neon short-circuiting, lethal and hot. Steam from subway grates roils from the Bowery to Harlem. Hell's Kitchen. Lids of garbage cans clanking alleys full of strays. Rain runneling iron-fronts in SoHo, 'cause you know it's *got* to be a dark and stormy one, wind battering hotel awnings. Umbrellas inside-out. Faces clouding windows on the cross-town bus. Yeasty refrigerator cartons full of homeless swell the avenues, damp eyes following you through slits. Witnessing the black coroner van, white lettering.

The death itself—envisioning it like you're there—drowsing in the steamy bathtub, his forehead waxy and soft. Eyelids slack. And white. Grime from the back of his neck staining the skin of water. Goblet of wine, red, on the rim of the tub. An expensive label. But he's not tasting it or anyone else anymore.

Those facts are a hell of a lot cleaner than the fantasy.

The fantasy isn't clean at all, why you like it: See, after he dumps you—you living in a crummy log cabin in Georgia—there you are all alone. Alone, but with your hard-core fantasy of a pearl snub-nose and a Barbara Stanwyck *love-and-murder-at-first-sight* glint in your eye. Like a metallic sliver in the cornea more like it. Hurting enough to make you mean. You walking into a poetry reading. Sure, you wish for Rick's American Café or a Grand Hotel-type setting—something—but you got to work with what you got to work with. So months, a year, the same celluloid image reels your mind: You, face veiled, red fingernails, matching lips, black sheath, fishnets, spikes, open-toed in case anyone notices, going with the 1940s original all the way. Walking toward the podium. Toward The Poet . . . his sports jacket a cape slung over his shoulders like a hip Bela Lugosi. He's reading verse, jazzy-like. Feeling cool. He doesn't know *how* cool.

Blam, blam, blam.

The no-good-lying son of a bitch.

The way it really happened, case anyone's wondering: You and he in a motel. Slumming. You've seen worse. But if *you've* been there, you know what it's like *at the time*, the way you're awash in unwashed sheets but pretending like crazy you're in some romantic detective caper penthouse suite. Think *The Thin Man* or any of its boozy sequels. Know what I'm saying? He's somehow looking straight at you with straying eyes. Lying through tarnished teeth. But you're not hearing or seeing. Instead you're believing he'll leave his wife. You'll leave your husband, splitting a marriage just like that. Move into his uptown apartment. The Big Apple. Easy as pie. What with *lips kissing like a fever / surfacing. Drunk, he hums midnight / blues, sound of subways tracking veins.*

Soon *you're* careening, too, 'cause of how he states it all nice. Like he means it. After all, you been looking so long you got to believe this shit's love.

Even though a rash on your heart says it's not.

And sure enough, before one valise in Georgia is packed, he pulls a fast one. A disappearing act.

All you got left is the *blam, blam, blam* fantasy . . . guys and dolls in the audience too stunned to move. Poet slumping at the podium like a weak line break, breaking. Red staining starched-and-pressed shirt, red like the wine on the rim of the bathtub. But trembling now—subway rumble vibrating wine, water. Rippling surfaces.

He was a boozer and a smoker. You got that right. I mean, if you were filling out a police report you'd include those little details because maybe it was booze and smoke caused his heart to misfire in the bathtub. Caused his heart to ignite all the girls before dousing them with ice water. Or gasoline. Let's face it, he was a womanizer, too. Yeah, write *that* in his *Times* obit. I'm thinking like what's-his-name actor in *Nocturne.*

Desire reeling like crazed / grackles cackling above slum rooftops— diesel promises billowing / asphalt's neon-slick / highway, air brakes hissing snakes. More like it.

But don't blame me. I ain't taking the rap, at least for this one. I'm five states away at the time, as the crow flies, the night in question. My prints don't mar the steam gauzing the mirror, his own lying eyes fading from his reflection. My alibi locked tight. Solid. End of story.

The beginning of the story shakes out like this:

Before the damp-sheets motel, chronologically speaking, you meet him at a writers' conference ninety-some miles from your home in Georgia. But admit it, kid, you attend that conference in the first place to track him—or someone. You even write a third-rate poem of your own to lure him—or someone. Third-rate best you can do at the time. On short notice.

But he says he loves the poem 'cause he's also hot on the trail of you—or something—so the poem, you could say, shreds in his hands. I mean, tell it like it is: It was never about poetry. Guess by now that goes without saying.

You mightily pretend it's about love. Don't much love your husband anymore. Husband doesn't much love you, *nada* in that department, so you're waiting for Bogart or Peck or Cary Grant. And The Poet—in what you can only call your *altered state of reality*—is close enough to pass. Or so you think at the time.

Sure you know now it was sex all the way.

But The Lie . . .

Don't forget that crucial detail.

"The *big* lie" as it's come to be known. The lie refuses to take a powder. Clings like a motherfucker around your neck. Sex is always sex. No two ways. But if only he'd *called* it sex, then you're just brokenhearted because of the disappearing act.

But he called it love. Called it marriage. Knowing that's what you needed to hear in order for you to unzip the black sheath, slide off the fishnets, slip off the spikes.

But after you unzipped and unslipped . . . he's back in New York City with the wife, you're back home with that husband, and after a couple of months the phone's dead as a metaphor, and the letters, which were supposed to be about love, go up in smut. But feel like frostbite. Color of blue lies. So blue we're talking indigo. Midnight.

That's when your fantasy kicks in, takes hold. Roots in your brain. Won't let go.

Not a fantasy that he leaves his wife. *Not* a fantasy that you'll finally pack up those valises and head to the bright lights, big city. His uptown apartment. That fantasy's for suckers. Losers. Which you no longer are.

Instead, the fantasy of you walking down the aisle and sure as shit not one in a church. But at that poetry reading, see. The audience not even noticing you at first, all absorbed in the verse of the poet, verse everyone *says* is art, but you know is cooler than steel. Not nearly as good as that *blam, blam, blam* fantasy of yours shredding the air.

It becomes your world, doesn't it, kid? That one image. A loop of celluloid spinning round and round in black and white. It won't stop, so *you* stop . . . living your own life that is. Lying in bed. Un-air-conditioned log cabin. Humidity dripping down walls. Mortar disintegrating, logs slipping from the frame. Sweat on your skin lasts so long it up and dries. Saw yourself as a girl stalking love. Thought you'd find it shamelessly flirting with him. Playing your own role in this Grade B, too. Feeling invincible. Till sirens start wailing. Till *you* start wailing.

Till you feel like blue smut ripped from pages of a magazine abandoned under someone's mattress where no one sleeps anymore.

That's when the fantasy veers from valentines to spiderwebs of glass cracking from stray bullets.

His final syllables clanging consonants, cornet, sax blasting / voweled brass / wedding bands cooling / tub water—heart hijacked and drowning / his lies / nightshade on your tongue.

His tongue.

You aren't the first gal who believed his promise, his lie. Or the last. So you probably feel a whole bunch of free-floating rage, too, as professional analysts might say. All his other girls, like you, embarrassing clichés, start falling out of the sooty woodwork. Gothic, if you're wondering. Minor chords of ruin. All the anger buzzing in your head, down your neck, through your heart, spiraling your left arm straight to the trigger finger.

Except you never pull it.

But ten years or so later, give or take, after the motel, he's snuffing out solo, instead. Breath dispersing like steam. Skin ossifying hard as white tile. Fingertips wrinkling. Eyes the color of the bottom of a rain puddle on asphalt. The cooling mirror reflecting a rectangular frame of the opposite wall. Blank.

Fine by you.

The vinyl record stutters at dusk, a needle scratching the last / note. The studs, a beatific chorus, eulogize him—while coffled girls mutely / wait to hear sod / thud wood, his chariot to exit / the show. Jacket caping his frigid silhouette.

Ready now. Final act. Last chapter. One diminishing verse. Your own unwrinkled fingers wave good-bye as if *you* picked up this hitch-hiking heart, dumping him at the last exit of Route 17.

You're still alive, surviving him and death, fueled, for now, on anger, pure as light.

Him. *He's* the only one without a home. Without a life. Without a name, which you withhold like evidence.

FLIRTING WITH THE BUTCHER

*vizard: in depreciatory use: a face or
countenance suggestive of a mask*

For example: "Addicts and cannibals
wear vizards, mingling among the living,
unrecognized, until it's too late."

I sit at a Formica table in Luby's Cafeteria, a glass of ice water before
me. I wonder how many calories are contained in each opaque cube.
Maybe more than in clear water. I stir it with a spoon. Maybe the
ice will melt quicker even in the frigid air-conditioning, freezing my
skin—the epidermis, the dermis, the hypodermis—in another hot
Atlanta summer.

Paul, with a plate of roast beef, mashed potatoes, gravy, and string
beans, sits across from me. I try to avoid looking at his dinner. The
scents from the chafing dishes in the self-serve line—which must be,
I'm convinced, upwards of five miles long—seem to slip down my
throat as if I'm swallowing the cafeteria whole. Melted sugar. Fried fat.
Overcooked vegetables. Undercooked meat. I imagine blood seeping
over the rim of carving boards and trailing across the linoleum floor
like evidence at a murder scene.

I've never met Paul before. He's interviewing me for my first 12-Step
group of Sex Addicts Anonymous. To be admitted into the private
inner sanctum of recovery, I must be deemed a safe (enough) person.

I want to be accepted; I want to be rejected.

To prove I am safe, that I will not attempt to seduce men who attend the meetings, I wear short-short denims, threads dangling from the hacked-off hems. I wear a too-tight tank top. Earlier, dressing, I believed these careless clothes to be asexual. How could such raggedy garments be misconstrued as seductive regardless of shortness or tightness? These aren't, after all, the shimmery glimmery clothes I wear to meet men in bars.

More of my skin shows than not. Especially in the fluorescent glare of Luby's. As if my body lies on a slab awaiting an autopsy. Nothing, however, would be found in my pristine stomach. Nothing would be found inside me at all.

I've lost so much weight my wedding ring slips up and down over my knuckle.

Paul wears a pressed shirt and khakis. He carves his beef into huge chunks and stabs it with his fork. Or that's what it looks like. Maybe, in reality, he's only cutting food into normal-sized bites. *Still*. Meat slides between his lips. His teeth are stained malarial yellow. From tobacco? Coffee? Tea? I wonder, if I licked them, would the stain get better or worse?

"When was the last time you acted out?" Paul asks. He already told me he hasn't had compulsive or emotionally unhealthy sex for over four years.

"Four weeks," I lie.

Last night.

He chews slowly. He watches me, unblinking. I know he knows I'm lying. I glance at the water now afraid even to drink. With one glass I'll feel bloated. Paul won't think I'm sexy with a distended stomach. I've been living on carrot strips and potato chips. The chips don't contain preservatives. Which must mean they have fewer calories. Food with less of *anything* in it is better than food with actual content. With food: less is more. With sex: more is less.

Earlier, as we pushed our trays along the serving line, mine remained empty. Paul asked why I wasn't hungry. I told him I'd already eaten. I used the word "already" loosely, open to interpretation, since I haven't eaten a full, regular meal in weeks. I don't know how to convey that if I refrain from eating or drinking, my body will evaporate. This is my own personal First Step. No body = no sex with dangerous men = no addiction.

Or no body = no disease. No body part to become infected, emotionally and/or physically. This, to me, is a reasonable plan for recovery. I don't consider starvation. Or, ironically, death.

"So you have an eating disorder, too." Paul nods at my water.

Busted.

"Most addicts are cross-addicted," he adds.

At the thought I'll have to attend *two* 12-Step groups, not just one, a tremor ripples my abdomen. I would rather hike the Gobi desert barefoot in a hair-blouse than attend two groups.

Or am *I* the desert? My heart feels dry, empty, desolate. I don't even know where the Gobi is. I want to ask Paul but, given the context, that might not make a good impression. Maybe he'll think I'm addicted to deserts.

I shake my head. I'm too exhausted even to lie about eating/not eating. He tells me that having an addictive personality is like that Three Stooges routine where one of the Stooges pushes in one dresser drawer only to have another drawer pop out. Meaning: You get one addiction under control and another surfaces.

Lately, I've been reading articles about the cannibal Jeffrey Dahmer. I want to explain to Paul that an addict is more like the Milwaukee serial killer than the Three Stooges. I don't. I'm enough in my right mind to know that my obsession with Dahmer is not a constructive topic of conversation.

But isn't cannibalism the ultimate eating disorder? If so, compared to Dahmer—and those heads he stored in freezers—mine is surely small potatoes, nothing to fret about. I don't consider that my own body is consuming itself.

Last night I picked up a man in a bar and went to the Thunderbird

Motel. I barely remember the man's face. I barely remember the sex. Men, sex . . . all have become indistinguishable. I stared at the motel ceiling, flecks of red paint mixed with white. Like sprinkles on vanilla ice cream. Or blood. I think the man hit me. *Did he hit me?* It must have been a mistake, or part of the sex. I awoke this morning, back in my bed at home, with a bruised smudge under my left eye. A souvenir. A memento. *Having a great time! Wish you were here!* I covered it with makeup. Only a lavender tint is visible. If Paul notices, he doesn't say. And my husband—husband #2—thank my Higher Power, is away on a research project for the summer.

I'm meeting Paul only because my therapist suggested (okay, *insisted*) I attend a 12-Step group. He won't see me individually if I continue to show up at his office "drunk" after acting out with a man—or hungover on men, sex, starvation—my personal drugs of choice. My therapist warned me I'm not emotionally strong enough—no addict is strong enough—to achieve sexual sobriety without the power of the group.

After Paul finishes eating, we head to the parking lot. Heat rises from asphalt while late-afternoon sunlight presses down on my head. My body is too frail to withstand the onslaught of weather. Any kind of weather. The inside of my un-air-conditioned vw bug steams. I roll down the windows and crank the engine.

I follow Paul's bright red Chevy toward the 12-Step meeting. I want to lose him in traffic. I don't want to lose him. If I lose him, I'll really only lose myself. Besides I have no place else to go. Or so the single healthy cell in my brain tells me. At any rate, the red of Paul's car is subtle as an ambulance's flashing lights. Fitting: I am, after all, my own one-woman emergency.

A couple of dozen people crowd into a hospital's activities room. I'm so thin, slim as a shadow, that I hide behind Paul as we enter. No one will see me. I find a seat in the back. Again the air-conditioning is too cold. Again I shiver. I should have brought a sweater, but I don't want to appear bulky as if I have actual meat on my bones. Even goosebumps on my bare arms swell the outline of my emaciated body.

Worse: Across the room, on a table, is a massive chocolate cake. "Congratulations Tom! 5 Years Sober" is written in neon-pink icing. I'm guessing if I ate the entire cake I'd consume 1,463,705 calories. Conservatively.

I also imagine if I eat a tiny piece, if I even lick a clean plastic fork, my stomach will convulse. The mere scent of sugar makes me dizzy, my muscles tight. I wonder what Jeffrey Dahmer ate for dessert. Is one body part sweeter than others?

STEP 1: WE ADMITTED WE WERE POWERLESS OVER SEX—THAT OUR LIVES HAD BECOME UNMANAGEABLE.

Paul stands to read the 12 Steps. I hear the words but don't know how they apply to me. Instead, I imagine unbuttoning his shirt. In reality I'm not the least attracted to him, to say nothing of the fact that if I proposition him I'll be thrown out of the meeting. But how else *to* see a man? Are men actually human? Actually people? Or merely objects?

I glance at the rough, industrial-strength carpeting. I imagine Paul and me having rough, industrial-strength sex.

I close my eyes. I don't want to admit anything. I have the right to remain silent.

STEP 2: A POWER GREATER THAN OURSELVES COULD RESTORE US TO SANITY.

Jeffrey Dahmer is a power greater than myself. I think about how many people he seduced, kidnapped, drugged, killed, grilled, steamed, fried, poached, broiled, fileted, baked, boiled, ate. I imagine how many body parts he froze to be defrosted later for midnight snacks.

At home my own freezer is empty. One sack of carrots wilts in the vegetable bin, and two bags of preservative-free potato chips stuff the cupboard.

My name is Tommy, and I'm a sex addict . . .

Hi, Tommy!

My name is Cheryl, and I'm a sex addict . . .

Hi, Cheryl!

The urgency or desperation of all the people in the room coalesces, no, coagulates. Although no one pays me any attention, still, it feels as if arms grab at me as if I'm an extra in the movie *Night of the Living Dead*. Or maybe it seems as if everyone here is after my soul, more like *Invasion of the Body Snatchers*. I want to tell them: All you'll find is an empty wound. A misplaced heart.

Or, to quote *Bride of Frankenstein*: "This heart's no good. I must have another."

Dear Jeffrey Dahmer,

Who wounded you: your mom? Dad? Relative? I can relate, believe me. My dad was his own special breed of familial cannibal, a predator who preyed on his own daughter, even though that seems like a million years ago. Or maybe it feels like yesterday. Anyway, I know where you're coming from: Do unto others, right? And because of the darkness in my father, of course I was attracted to the darkness of boardwalks, didn't know how to take care of myself, was drawn to the confusion of love/sex with Dr. Blue Convertible. To say nothing of The Poet. So this is where we end up, right? I just wish you'd attended a 12-Step group before you were arrested.

My name is Jeffrey, and I'm a cannibal.

Hi, Jeffrey!

Oh, well, it's all just blood over the damned at this point, so to speak, whether we speak or not.

You May Already Be a Winner!

Last month I had a vision: I *knew*, with 100 percent certainty, *absolutely*, without a doubt, that the Publishers Clearing House Prize Patrol van would stop at my house on June 30. Balloons! Flowers! Champagne! A big cardboard check for ten million dollars! I'd filled out the contact card with my name and address, so they'd easily find me. On the card was my own personal entry number. I did everything right. Played by the rules for once.

No purchase necessary.

I was convinced, nevertheless, magazine purchases would increase my chances. I randomly selected colorful stickers of magazine covers, licked the glue on the backs (how many calories?), and stuck them on entry slips: *Newsweek, Prevention, U. S. News and World Report, Allure.*

I was allured by the caption "You Won"! I ignored the small type below claiming "if you return your entry form and it displays the winning number." *If.* I refused to consider any *if*s, *and*s, or *but*s. I believed I would win the sweepstakes as completely and compulsively as I believed that sex with dangerous men equals love . . . as fervently as I believed that ice water is a well-balanced meal.

How difficult to distinguish the difference between sex and love. Win or lose. What's real. What's fake.

I waited by the door all day on June 30 watching for the Prize Patrol. In the end whatever prize you win, is *you*.

I feel faint. Just the sight of the cake is emetic. I bend over, palms on either side of my face. I will not speak. I will not say *my name is . . .* What *is* the name of this person hunching into herself?

Maybe, however, a moral inventory would reveal I am *not* an addict.

Maybe my obsession with Jeffrey Dahmer is completely normal. Maybe I will still win the sweepstakes.

Cheryl is saying she had sex with three men last night. She feels like a slut. A whore. She wears a tan linen skirt and a white frilly blouse. She looks as if she just took her kids to school. She looks as if she just returned home from the grocery store. She doesn't look like a sex addict. No one here does.

Well, maybe I do.

STEP 5: WE ADMITTED TO GOD, TO OURSELVES, AND TO ANOTHER HUMAN BEING THE EXACT NATURE OF OUR WRONGS.

Dear Jeffrey Dahmer,

You don't know me. But I want to tell you all about...

STEP 6: WE WERE ENTIRELY READY TO HAVE GOD REMOVE ALL THESE DEFECTS OF CHARACTER.

Dear Jeffrey Dahmer,

I saw a photo of you in your orange jumpsuit. Orange is not a good color for you. Once I saw a picture of you when you were a little boy. You wore a blue shirt. Do you remember it? I wonder what happened to it. What happened to you? At what point in your life did someone leave you behind? Is this about abandonment? For you? For me?

We must be ready to have our defects removed like a diseased organ, an appendix, say, or a heart.

STEP 7: WE HUMBLY ASKED HIM TO REMOVE OUR SHORTCOMINGS.

Instead of shortcomings maybe I suffer from a version of locked-in syndrome—which makes people uncommunicative while in their own bodies—mutely looking out. They aren't able to speak or express themselves.

I feel as if the real "me" is locked inside an addict. How can I say *my name is*... when I can't speak? Or when I no longer know my real name? Or I *know* it, but it no longer describes me. I am no longer me. My body or my soul has been snatched. Or devoured.

Dear Jeffrey Dahmer,

Do you feel as if the real you is locked inside the body of a cannibal? Did you first gnaw on yourself like an appetizer then, famished, set the table with plates, knives, forks before starting on others for the entrée?

STEP 8: WE MADE A LIST OF ALL PERSONS
WE HAD HARMED, AND BECAME WILLING
TO MAKE AMENDS TO THEM ALL.

Last month I made a list of Jeffrey Dahmer's 17 victims. I copied names on a yellow legal pad. I considered each person's body parts: chewed, hacked, frozen, sealed in containers of brine. How long did it take him to polish off an arm, a leg, a kidney, a lung?

I once tried to list all the men with whom I had sex. My Lucky Number 17 was a guy who wore bifocals. I wondered if he saw two of me until he removed them and placed them on the nightstand. Is there a sober me? Or only an addict me? I had an irrational desire to smash his glasses, although I didn't.

STEP 9: WE MADE DIRECT AMENDS TO SUCH PEOPLE
WHEREVER POSSIBLE, EXCEPT WHEN TO DO SO
WOULD INJURE THEM OR OTHERS.

I glance around the room. All these strangers. I don't know anyone. No one knows me. It's impossible to know anyone. Ever. It's impossible to know me. Yet these people want me to confess my darkest secrets, a darkness that freezes my spine. Safer to have sex with men who don't *want* to know me. Kissing lips that feel skinless. Pressed hard against a mattress by an anonymous body. Stumbling out of motel rooms feeling more weightless than when I entered.

To whom or what should I make amends:

To all the motel rooms I abandoned. To all the canned goods I never bought or bought and let expire. I'm sorry about my cat's empty food bowl. Sorry for the dead plant in its macramé hanger. Sorry for my smudged makeup that at the beginning of the evening—before the bar, before the motel—looked so pretty. I'm sorry about underwear abandoned in sheets in men's apartments. Ditto for all the lost buttons. Apologies to each sock that lost, due to my own negligence, its mate. I'm sorry I'd rather flirt with the man behind the meat counter in the grocery store than eat beef sliced off cows that I might have passed in a pasture two days ago. I'm really, really sorry about the cows—what happens to them—whether I flirt with the butcher or not.

Dear Jeffrey Dahmer,

I regret I didn't meet you before you were arrested. I imagine you wandering those midnight Milwaukee streets. You pause at a stop sign spying a young man. Could I have stopped you? Could you have stopped me? Power is in the group, after all.

Or maybe nothing, no one, could have saved you.

Sure, you were abandoned one way or another as a child. But what about your victims? You ate them because you were afraid they'd leave you. Paradoxically, they did—because you ate them.

And you abandoned yourself.

Have I abandoned myself? I thought my parents, my sister, the white stallion in the West Indies, my piano, the Poet, the doctor in the blue convertible—all of them—abandoned me. And maybe they did. But now I've lost myself, my true self, to this addiction . . . addiction, a form of suicide, another diagnosis for death.

Jeff, as we make amends to others, do we also make amends to ourselves?

A woman with curly hair touches my shoulder. A warm finger against cold skin. I'm surprised I feel it. I'm scared I feel it. It means I'm still alive. She tells me her name. I immediately forget it. She says she'd like to be my sponsor. She hands me a paper plate with a slice of cake.

At first, convinced I really am suffering from locked-in syndrome, I only blink my eyes. As her warm finger continues to press my shoulder, I'm able to shake my head. *No, I don't want a sponsor. No, I don't want cake. No, I don't want . . .*

"The first time is tough," she says. She sits beside me. "My first meeting I left here and had sex in, like, twenty minutes."

I nod my head.

"I'm glad you're here," she says. "The worst thing is to feel you're going through this all alone." She forks a tiny piece of cake and holds it toward me. "Eat something," she says.

"That's okay," I say. "Maybe tomorrow."

STEP 10: WE CONTINUED TO TAKE PERSONAL INVENTORY AND WHEN WE WERE WRONG PROMPTLY ADMITTED IT.

Item one: Jeffrey Dahmer.

Item two: Everything else.

STEP 11: WE SOUGHT THROUGH PRAYER AND MEDITATION TO IMPROVE OUR CONSCIOUS CONTACT WITH GOD, PRAYING ONLY FOR KNOWLEDGE OF HIS WILL FOR US AND THE POWER TO CARRY THAT OUT.

Okay, Jeffrey Dahmer is not exactly god but also not exactly human. He pushed addiction to the nth degree and beyond. He stalked straight out of Normal, left it behind, and entered his own State of Being with his own merciless theology.

He no longer cared.

He never made amends.

He left bones in attics and clumps of hair in basements. It didn't/ doesn't matter to him. Nothing mattered or matters. Jeffrey Dahmer: *How did you arrive at a place of being where you ate someone's heart for dinner and murdered again simply for a second helping?*

"What?" the woman says.

"Nothing," I say, scared I may have said Dahmer's name out loud. Not a good First or Eleventh Step to recovery, I suspect.

I walk out of the room, out of the hospital. I stand in the parking lot. The heat of day still steams from asphalt. I could return to the meeting. I could get sober. And I will. But not now. Not yet. I wonder how many times, if ever, Jeffrey Dahmer said that to himself.

STEP 12: HAVING HAD A SPIRITUAL AWAKENING AS THE RESULT OF THESE STEPS, WE TRIED TO CARRY THIS MESSAGE TO SEX ADDICTS, AND TO PRACTICE THESE PRINCIPLES.

I sit on the bumper of my vw. The metal beneath my legs warms my air-conditioned skin. If I drive to Milwaukee, would I be allowed into the jail to see Jeffrey Dahmer? I could bring him a hamburger. If I fed him a bite, slipped it between his lips, scented with my skin, would he swallow it? Would he eat just the hamburger and leave my fingertips intact?

My forefinger feels sticky from a smudge of cake icing. I want to wipe it on my shorts. I want to taste it. I want to do both. I'm afraid to move. I am paralyzed as if any decision, thought, action will be wrong. If I return to the 12-Step meeting, I could get the phone number of the curly-haired woman who wants to be my sponsor. I could drive to a bar and pick up a man. I could bring him to the Thunderbird Motel, its neon sign, a tomahawk, chopping night to shreds. I could drive home.

I press the icing against my mouth. My stomach rumbles with desire.

Of course I won't visit Jeffrey Dahmer in jail. He is, after all, only, merely, another obsession or distraction in order for me to ignore more pressing issues: ironically, the reasons I fear death, as well as the state of my life.

The aftereffects, like a sonic boom, of the man under the boardwalk. That I gave birth to something inhuman. Un-human. Too.

Dahmer once said he was a serial killer because he had to keep repeating the pattern. The act of seducing, killing, eating was never as satisfying or perfect as the fantasy of the act in his head.

He never found what he was looking for.

Jeff...

My actual encounters of acting out with men are never as perfect as the fantasy images, either. That's why I, too, am a serial seducer. More: I keep thinking, hoping, I'll find love (life) in the Thunderbird Motel even though I never do.

Jeffrey, I know where you're coming from, believe me.

So little separates us. A heart here. A kidney there. A liver in the oven. But, one way or another, none of those men we seduce survive long enough for true love to nourish us.

Are our wounds, all the abandonments, so deep they—or we—are comatose? Emotionally, physically, spiritually.

Cars stream along Cobb Parkway, headlights, taillights, sweeping into a world of the living. For now I'm free in the night. A warm drizzle dampens the street. I get in my car. I turn on the windshield wipers. I follow the taillights of the car ahead of me, mindlessly, as if it's my Higher Power. It will lead me to Heaven or maybe to a home where I don't live.

The wipers slash back and forth.

I lose my way in the city. I'm on an unknown street in an unfamiliar neighborhood. Most of the houses are dark. If I ring someone's doorbell would they let me in or would they lock their doors and windows, dial 911, after one fleeting glance at this emaciated monster?

But no I'm not, after all, the Bride of Dahmer.

At the end of the day—or more likely the night—I understand the difference between fantasy and reality, obsession and normal thought. I know I have only this one heart. Tomorrow or the next day or the following day at the latest, I will return to the 12-Step group. I will offer up my irreplaceable, no-good heart for repair.

THE THREE FATES AND
THE BAREFOOT ANGELS

We live in a house on a street with an ordinary name. An ordinary house, save for butcher paper taped across window panes. Its coordinates, however, spread across a map's axis. All the city streets and rural lanes.

Do you want to know where you are going? Angels don't wear socks, we are able, at this juncture, to reveal.

Where am I? Where am I? you call out. These words reverberate across the cool skim of consciousness.

Where am I?

And if we were to be so bold to respond: Might we divulge that you stumbled slipping out of bed? How banal. But it's all banal, we must say.

Have I nothing? No photos? No jewelry?

We wipe slivers of sweat from your forehead and reply *nothing*.

Why am I here?

Because you couldn't arise from the floor.

It is as if we speak in foreign tongues. We conjugate verbs backward. No one understands. We live in constant misunderstandings. Misdirections. Miscommunications. The toll it takes.

We play purple shadows, the sound of a fever, on your shoulders. We're the only ones who know how close you are.

We're the only ones who know your other name.

FATE 3   ATROPOS

cuts the thread of life with a pair of shears to decide how someone dies

AT THE TERMINAL GATE

Immedicable: untreatable

For example: "I turn another page in my 1972 *Hammond's
Contemporary World Atlas* searching for locations, answers,
refusing to believe life's inconveniences are immedicable."

My grandfather dies. My family and I fly on Caribair from St. Thomas
to Puerto Rico before boarding a Pan American Clipper to New York
City, *en route* to Los Angeles, to attend his funeral. I sit by the window
expecting my grandfather to float past. No one explains "death" or
"funerals," so my child-mind glimpses snippets of information or misin-
formation. *What is death?* My imagination creates its own expectations.

My forehead, pressed to the window, warms. Sunlight dazzles silvery
wings. My hazel-colored eyes search cloudy spindrifts. I don't want
to miss my grandfather float past. Will he be wearing his gray suit,
white shirt, black tie? Or will he be draped in a white robe like Jesus?
I've heard my grandfather's a Communist, which sounds academic
and boring. I wonder if he might carry heavy books. He'll need reading material for the lengthy journey. Maybe he's returning to Russia,
where he was born. Maybe when you die you visit your ancestors, an
otherworldly vacation.

Neither my parents nor my sister cry, so I don't anticipate a sad
event. Besides I barely know him. We live far away. My only clear
memory is playing pick-up sticks with him on the worn-gray carpet in
my grandparents' apartment. He sat beside me and handed me a fistful

of sticks colorful as a bouquet. I opened my fingers. They spiraled into a heap. How many red, blue, yellow sticks can you pick up without moving another one? How careful do you have to be to win?

I am asleep by the time we reach California. I never saw my grandfather outside the airplane window. He must have floated past while I slept.

I enter the synagogue, trailing my sister and parents. Across the foyer is the casket. I don't yet see him inside. But how *can* he be inside when, no doubt, he's emigrating back to Russia?

I'm also confused because this temple is unlike the one at home in St. Thomas: No soft layer of sand covers the floor. During Saturday morning services I slide from the pew to play in the sand, since the mumbling of the rabbi bores me. Here, however, the floor is marble.

And there's that casket.

Behind me someone whispers: *It should be closed.*

I'm pushed forward. My black patent leather shoes barely touch the ground. The room smells of overripe lilies. The scent scares me. The air should smell blue, like air, like space. I stand on tiptoe peering at waxy features. His bald head is no longer slick but dull as ash with a fringe of white hair. Here he is present. Yet he appears absent.

My grandfather is dead, yet I feel as if *I* am in the box. Not the physical me, but the soul part of me, which first died after building that toy paper house with my father—that paper doll in its jewelry casket.

I don't recall falling, tripping, or fainting. But here I am face down on the cold marble floor, a mosaic of blues and greens. Hands, just as cold, lift me, setting me on a chair. My mouth tastes like a sliver of sodium beneath my tongue. I feel as if I swallowed a rock even as I'm utterly weightless, my lungs flat as cloth napkins pressed and starched. There's not enough air in the temple to breathe. Instead I inhale breath exhaled by my grandfather at the moment he died. I look down at my body that seems strangely distant. I want to witness my blood rivering through veins. I can't. I press my hand to my heart. Is it beating? Am I here? Am I me?

When my family returns to St. Thomas after the funeral, I fall asleep. I sleep so deeply I must, at times, be unconscious. I don't leave my bed for three months. I can't. I feel as if the weakest bone in my body snapped and, without it, my entire frame falls limp. West Indian heat coils my matted hair. My grandfather's shadow—all my shadowy Russian ancestors—hover over me in this long sleep.

How did I arrive here, *here,* from my ancestral Russia? How did a "pre-me" depart from frozen Russian steppes to appear in the tropical Caribbean? I couldn't have followed a straight line to reach this point in my existence. Time and space are circular, not linear. In this memory, close to nonexistence, my senses are heightened during moments when I'm hypnogogic: not quite awake; not quite asleep.

Am I brought to the hospital? Is there a diagnosis? Maybe the diagnosis is that my memory contains my dead ancestors. My first encounter with death, therefore, occurs before my birth, my fear of death beginning before I am born. I contain a collective, cellular memory that's weighty, feverish, complicated. Their lives—their deaths—are mine.

Maybe, then, this illness isn't physical. Maybe this pseudo-death is metaphoric, is meant to warn me to be vigilant, aware of everything around me—the past and the present—the conscious and the unconscious me.

The sickness passes. I walk onto the verandah overlooking the Caribbean. The red hibiscus bloom, as always. Bougainvillea still explode like fireworks over whitewashed walls. The West Indian sun, at dusk, still spills into the water so quickly I almost hear the splash. Bats swoop low in the trees.

The world is unchanged. All is as I remember. This is reassuring. Surely, then, nothing and no one has died. If someone *had* died, the hibiscus would wilt. The bougainvillea would faint, sliding off the walls. I would still smell overripe lilies.

Death is so big it's not possible for the world to continue unchanged if someone dies, if someone is utterly and totally obliterated.

My grandfather didn't die.

He simply disappeared.

Just as he once disappeared from Russia leaving behind one hundred leagues of misery, leaving our ancestors who didn't escape—their memories thin sounds on a balalaika—Black Sea ice frozen to the frayed hems of their souls.

But maybe they're not gone, either.

I examine old photographs—daguerreotypes, tintypes. Year after year these relatives seem gaunter, yet more real. Women, cameo brooches fastened over their hearts, sit on horsehair sofas. Men stand behind them: faces stern, arms crossed. Not all their stories survive, although some do, enough to be tangible, enough to keep them seeming less dead than dead.

My father's father owned a tavern. Or worked in a tavern? Could a Jew actually *own* a business in Kiev? He escaped Russia after being conscripted into the czar's army, sailed to Ellis Island, eventually found his way to Chicago, where he owned a dry cleaning establishment.

As a young man my father earned money in that business in order to attend the University of Chicago. He loved to iron, and I inherited this ability. In high school I pressed oxford shirts like this: I began with the collar, proceeded to the yoke, the sleeves, the back, the front placket, the sides. I stretched the seams flat as the iron smoothed wrinkles. I sprinkled the material with droplets of water.

I loved the hiss of escaping steam. Once, ironing while I watched television (I had lowered the board so I could sit down), the iron slipped onto my thigh. It left a vaguely spaceship-shaped burn.

My father called ironing *"bigeling."* Is *bigeling* a Yiddish word? A made-up word? I don't know. It doesn't matter. What matters is my love of the word—the memory it evokes—its spiritual DNA—the steamy scent of it, the truest truth.

Even though I never again see my flesh-and-blood grandfather, I think of him as merely misplaced or missing, having traveled, perhaps, too far afield. Or his body has been transformed into flecks of lint. He's as hidden as a secret contained in the shaft of a feather, the nucleus of a rock, the shape of the sea.

But maybe I'm wrong. Maybe the scope of death means it's everywhere. I imagine his bones collapsing like a pile of pick-up sticks. No, I refuse to believe that.

The spaceship scar from the burn never fully disappears—maybe nothing does. Everything we do ripples through space-time in ways that contribute to memory, a trail I follow. In the end I don't want to just sit on the launching pad waiting for takeoff, waiting to depart the terminal. I want the memories and stardust that comprise me to shine.

MISS ROUTE 17'S
OWN GRACELAND

appetency: a longing or desire

piepowder: a traveler or itinerant trader

For example: "I am a piepowder of appetency."

I'm too old to run away from home. But here I am in my silver Toyota Camry, on I-196, before merging onto I-57, driving from Grand Haven, Michigan, to Galveston, Texas. Soon I'm somewhere in the middle of nowhere downstate Illinois, surrounded by a gray October sky and miles of fields of something or nothingness. Maybe last summer's crop of corn or soybeans once flourished in the horizon-defying fields, but the season for green growth is way past, just as I am way past. But past what?

My (soon to be ex-) husband and I moved to Michigan from Georgia one week ago. Traumatized by the move, I tossed a few clothes in a duffel and hit the road. The salt water of the Gulf of Mexico calls to the salty water that comprises much of the human body. Much of mine. My house in Grand Haven is located only a few blocks from Lake Michigan, but I don't understand the scentless lake. No salty air; seaweed doesn't wash ashore. All you'd find on the other side is unexotic Wisconsin. The waves on the other side of the Gulf of Mexico, however, lap against Cuba or Colombia. In any event, the urge to stand on the beach in Galveston is one of those separated-at-birth urges, an urge to return Home, even though I only lived in Galveston about seven years.

The disorientation of the move to Michigan is exacerbated because I suspect that, even though I moved to be with my husband, he is about to leave me. So I'm also driving to Galveston to spend hours in a car where no one can find me . . . even though, ironically, no one is looking for me. I need to be alone in preparation for *really* being alone, soon enough.

Elton John's *Greatest Hits* CD blares, his voice filling the empty spaces in the car. I especially love the song "I'm Still Standing." Also ironic because I'm not. Not only am I physically sitting, but I feel flattened by this move to the flat Midwest. When my husband first announced he'd gotten a job offer to teach at a college in West Michigan, I opened my outdated *Hammond's Contemporary World Atlas* to locate the state somewhere north of Georgia. Not that I particularly felt at home in Georgia, but I knew I wouldn't feel at home in Michigan, either. Which is the root of the problem, I suppose. The tantalizing idea of Home is illusory. For me, there is no one single place to stand, to stake a claim, and demand this spot as mine. Except, against all odds, I'm hoping to find such a spot on the beach in Galveston.

At least this is what I tell myself mile after mile, hour after hour, passing those fields of nothingness. My plan doesn't extend past the one moment of standing on the beach.

In short, I'm now headed south to find out *what comes next.*

I slouch in the car seat, my left arm pressed against the closed window ledge. *I'm still standing. I'm still standing.* After listening to the song dozens of times, I memorize the lyrics and sing along as loudly as possible.

The first time I ran away from home, I lived in St. Thomas. I wrapped up two quarters, a mango, and a hair ribbon in a hankie. Sucking on a short joint of sugarcane, I walked down Blackbeard's Hill to the harbor, abruptly stopping at the boat dock. Which is where I realized the inherent flaw in trying to run away from home when you live on an island. Boundaries. I was hemmed in by lacy foam. I had no intention of swimming across the Caribbean to the other side because I'd surely drown. I simply wanted to run away. Back then I was trapped. Nowhere to go.

Now I'm running *to* an island. Luckily, Galveston is accessible by a concrete causeway, which I yearn to race across, landing in the soft humid pillow of tropical air. Years after leaving Galveston, I miss it. Or miss something.

Still on I-57, I pass exits for Manteno and Kankakee. I am dazzled by options, so many places one *could* run away to. Then, after veering onto I-55 in Tennessee, I see a sign for Memphis. *Why not?* Graceland. I've never seen it. I've never wanted to see it. I don't particularly like Elvis Presley. But here it is, presented to me. So, yes, why not?

I pull into the parking lot of Graceland. Hoards of tourists stream past the airplane named *Lisa Marie* heading toward the white-columned mansion. I funnel along as if sliding down a chute into a make-believe land. *This is where Elvis Presley, the King of Rock 'n' Roll, lived.* I want to be gripped by the hype. But, upon entering, my breath slows rather than quickens. I slog past fifties-style gold drapes and white sofas. I enter the Jungle Room resembling a post-annihilated rain forest. Or a Polynesian smashup of dusty wood carvings and a green shag carpet. You *could* say it's kitsch. But it's not kitschy enough to be kitsch. Mainly, it's sad. Elvis's white-caped suit seems a bit the worse for wear. I want to apologize to it for viewing it well past its prime.

Which is how I feel. Past my prime.

I end up outside by Elvis's grave. This plot of land is called the Meditation Garden. It's anything but. Elvis Aaron Presley's grave is outlined by neon-colored flowers and American flags. Other graves surround his, his mother and father, perhaps. But how can I meditate amid crowds of sobbing women? I feel like weeping, too, but not because of Elvis's untimely drug-induced demise. Rather, because I fear my own: untimely or otherwise. Death is death any way you encounter it.

Still, why did Elvis hasten his? Maybe Graceland, while appearing to be his sanctuary, wasn't. Maybe *he* should have run away from home. He had so much. But maybe the wealth and fame of "much" was, in fact, too "little." Or the wrong kind of "much," as reflected in this tacky, trademarked shrine to his life.

That evening, I'm caught in a thunderstorm that washes away vision. I can't even see taillights ahead of me. I slow to about thirty miles per hour looking for an exit to a motel. The windshield wipers only blur the glass. The sky bleeds pure water, the car hydroplaning. I'm not scared. It simply feels like part of the adventure of running away from home. If you're going to do something significant, then floods and plagues are part of the package.

I finally find an exit that advertises a motel. I don't exactly know where I am in that the sign is merely the name of a road, and the motel is not even as unswanky as a Motel 6. It's a nonbrand, cinderblock, out-of-the-way-last-chance place to (hopefully) survive a night away from home. I now wish I remembered the name of the motel, but I suspect it wouldn't be kitschy enough to be cool, either. Nor is this a night for metaphors. Tonight, rain is merely rain. A random motel is simply that. At least that's what I thought back then.

I stumble from the car and am drenched before I reach the unprotected entrance. A teenage girl watches a small black-and-white television behind the registration desk. Silently, I hand her a credit card. No need to inquire about vacancies or price. We both know it doesn't matter how much it costs since I'm staying here at any rate. Her fingernails are ragged. Her lipstick is mostly licked off. From a kitchenette behind her is the scent of burned popcorn and too-sweet caramel. My body seems to be vibrating, unable to relinquish the motion of the car. My head spins. I grip the counter. The clerk sighs as she hands me the receipt to sign. Her movements are slow, somnambulistic. I almost ask her if she wants to run away with me. However, I suspect that *this,* right here in this motel, is *her* home, or as good as it's going to get for her. In this middle-of-the-night-drenched-night we seem to be the last two people on earth.

My damp palm smudges the receipt. She doesn't care. She slides a plastic key chain toward me and points toward the left out the door. There is no interior hallway to reach the room. I don't return to my car for my duffel. I run to the room. Jam the key into the door knob. I enter an anonymous space I've encountered a million times before. And, in the end, not so different from Graceland except in size and the color of the shag carpet—burnt orange. I've stumbled into a cliché, but clichés have their own appeal if you're in the right frame of mind. I almost am.

I yank off my wet clothes. I turn on the hot water in the shower. I close the bathroom door so the room fills with steam. I unwrap a miniature bar of no-name soap. I stand under the spray until my skin resembles a first-degree burn. In this early fall weather, I don't even have the satisfaction of watching summer sweat and dirt swirl down the drain. It's as if I'm a ghost stained red from the scorching water. Red, but still invisible. No one can see me here since, as I've said, no one's looking. I told my husband I was driving to Galveston, so he wouldn't call Missing Persons. Still, I feel a mild dissatisfaction that you can run away from home and know that no one's searching.

I dry off with a towel the size of a washcloth. Then another one. I pull on my underwear and bra. I wrap the faded chenille bedspread around my shoulders and sit on the bed. No dry clothes since I left them in the car. Then I remember my very first suitcase when I was a young child: navy blue, hard-sided. You pushed two brass buttons and the snaps popped open. Inside, a silky mauve lining with little pockets held treasures I found on vacations: shells, or beach glass, or a pine cone, or a plastic ring from a gumball machine. That suitcase always smelled of memories and must.

I missed dinner—too focused on the rain. I dig through my purse for something to eat. All I find is a package of spearmint gum. I chew two pieces and trick my stomach into believing this is food. After the flavor dissipates, I swallow the gum. Wrapped in the spread I lie back on the pillow.

My body reels with the motion of the car as if it's still speeding forward. It's as if I don't know how to stop—have never known how to stop. I try to remember all the streets, roads, interstates, routes, highways that led me *here*. All the swerves and exits, all the choices to turn here or here or there. I have made right turns, left turns, U-turns, wrong turns. My house in Michigan is perfectly fine, so I don't know why I can't accept it as *my* house. No more need to seek, travel, search. Yet here I am, still restless.

Late the next morning, now on 1-40, I glide across state lines into Arkansas. On the spur of the moment, I turn toward Hope, the birthplace of President Bill Clinton. Once you've been to Graceland, I figure you must visit Hope as well. I'm so buzzed and disoriented from driving, however, all I find in Hope are shops filled with Bill Clinton souvenirs. I buy a coffee mug. It's black with a blue silk-screened image of Clinton wearing sunglasses, playing the sax. "The Cure for the Blues," it reads. I don't seek out Clinton's birthplace. I return to the car in a haze of interstate wind and movement, a kind of hollowness on the cusp of displacement. Or perhaps displacement on the cusp of hollowness. Initially, I meant to drive straight from Grand Haven to Galveston, but now I'm meandering into side trips that seemed to promise so much.

Back in the car, heading toward Texarkana, I see what I want to believe is an eagle—though it isn't—perched on a wood fence. I want it to be an American bald eagle because that would be a good detail for my adventure. *Running away from home I discovered Graceland, Hope, and an American bald eagle.* I slow the car to watch it. *Still* not an eagle. I want it to look at me. It doesn't. It's quietly leading its bird life, while I'm busy seeking my person life.

Still I drive—the bird now many miles behind me. I stop at gas stations, Burger Kings, bathrooms, one after another, my knees humming with motion, anxious whenever I stop the car. The tires root me to the earth as much as they hurtle me forward to a destination beyond the horizon. My body has always felt unsettled, anxious, ready to move as if my veins themselves are miniature interstates, blood rushing from my neck to my stomach, the crook of an arm to a finger, from knee to a toe, never stopping. I drive on blind faith that these highways will eventually arrive at some point that's real—one that answers seemingly unanswerable questions—so that I'm no longer merely following lines on a map.

Finally, late afternoon, I stand on the beach in Galveston. I kick off my sneakers and roll up the hems of my black denims. Water washes over my feet. The breeze dampens my hair. Later, I will check into a honky-tonk motel on the honky-tonk seawall. Later, alone, I will eat a shrimp po' boy on the South Jetty overlooking the Gulf. My first ex-husband no longer lives here. There are no friends to visit. I do not return to renew acquaintances or sightsee. I drive over fifteen hundred miles simply to stand on the beach.

But not just stand on *this* beach.

For I am also a young girl still standing on the shore of the Caribbean. My arms smell of tropical heat, a bruised mango. I am also a teenage girl still standing on the shore of the Atlantic Ocean in New Jersey, smelling of sweet summer sweat and bubblegum—that innocently reckless teenage scent.

I'm also the twenty-six-year-old Galveston "me" who once lived here in a hail of sorrow, a sorrow too intense to carry all of it with me when I moved away. Now I've returned to reclaim it. Or, more exactly, reclaim *me*. Reclaim all my different bodies now hopefully morphing together until I am whole. A completed me. But I'm quite sure that's more a wish than a reality.

I remain on the beach watching the day slide below the horizon. *Still standing.* A quest requires a destination. This is mine—at least in the short term. A quest doesn't necessarily require that you gain insight and knowledge. It doesn't even require that you return home—despite Odysseus and the whole Odyssey thing. Although, bending to practicality, I did return to that Michigan house where my things and my soon-to-be-ex-husband were stored.

My heart is perhaps too deeply connected to too many places to ever find a physical home that resonates with me. Instead, like a hermit crab, I carry my home with me—an emotional and spiritual home scavenged from the past.

If this is so, then ultimately I am always at home—with myself, with my longings, and with my fear of death.

I want to claim that I saw and understood all of this in that one translucent dusk while contemplating the Gulf of Mexico.

I did not.

It is only later, only at the very moment, this eternal and fleeting *now* in which I write this—as each word is considered and either kept or discarded like so many seashells—that I build for myself my own place of hope and grace.

MEMORABILIA

My Guardian Devils and the Phantom of the Opera Gloves

orison: a prayer

For example: "I whisper an orison over inherited
objects to ensure their power won't be effaced
or erased over disputed provenance or time."

I wander around airless rooms of my neighbor's house in Grand Haven.
Dirt from the shoes of dozens of strangers smudge the worn wall-
to-wall carpet, probably not replaced since the 1950s. The estate sale
began at 7:30 this morning. It's about nine now, and the detritus of
the two widows' lives has been picked over. Sets of dainty teaspoons
lie askew on an antique oak table. Clothes, from-who-knows-what
decade, barely cling to hangers as shoppers yank things from closets.
There are garments labeled "dusters" from when women dusted. They
could also be called "house dresses" or what my Jewish grandmothers
called *schmattes*.

The beds are neatly made with faded chenille bedspreads. I wonder
if the man running the estate sale plumped the pillows or whether
this duty was performed by the last widow before she died. The beds
appear to be awaiting the women's return or waiting to welcome their
ghostly spirits.

I leave the bedrooms immediately.

Their possessions will ultimately be spread around the city, the state,
other states, and States of Being. Once their possessions take up residence with new owners, will an essence of the widows accompany

their things or be left behind? Once sold, will the provenance line be broken as if these women never existed, all trace of them erased from the human continuum?

Except *I* will be the one to remember them. *And I will tell.*

I'm not here to buy. I'm here to ensure the widows are sufficiently dead, their souls dispersed as their things, so that it's safe once again to enter the backyard of my house.

During the year my second husband and I lived together in Grand Haven, he befriended these two neighbor ladies, widowed mother and daughter. He helped them carry groceries, rearrange furniture, move heavy objects. So after my husband suddenly left, they seemed to miss him more than I missed him, even though I found myself alone in Michigan, my friends still back in Georgia. They were also angry at *me* instead of at my husband who left them. For example, they refused to greet me when I weeded the row of tea rose bushes beside their fence.

They also complained when my sprinkler inadvertently sprayed their property. They never objected when my husband set the sprinkler on our roses, but now they yelled, *You're splashing our garden tools!* I tried to regulate the arc so not a drop contaminated their yard. Yet wayward droplets inevitably chevyed on the breeze. Their scolds turned to shrieks when my sprinkler doused the edge of their patio.

Soon I was afraid to water, period. I snuck out at night hoping they wouldn't notice. But they knew the instant I crept onto my porch. I turned the knob on the outdoor faucet, hurried back inside, and closed the door. Night after night, the summer moon burned while neighborhood lights extinguished one by one, except theirs. I watched their silhouetted forms watching *me*, my house, as they peered out through sheer curtains.

One day in frustration I cranked the sprinkler full throttle. I stood in the yard, waiting, as water streamed across the roses onto their property. Their door banged open. Cracked voices snarled: *You're a bitch who lost her husband!*

And right there in front of them, without turning off the sprinkler, I yanked up all twenty-two tea rose bushes my husband carefully planted. I dumped them on the ground, petals pink as icing dissolving on a wedding cake.

Now I am the only one remaining in our two ancient houses. I know I'm better off without my husband, yet my part of the neighborhood seems empty without the melodrama of sudden abandonment, without the despair suffered by the widows after my husband left them. But I refuse to consider any scenario in which my husband or the widows return—even though our two backyards are now sprinkled with longing and loss.

One day, soon after, I have to go downstairs to the basement, the one part of the house I dread. Slowly I ease open the door. Damp air smelling of crumbling bricks, rusty pipes, and cobwebs rushes up at me. I feel as if I enter a ghost story: If the widows are lying in wait, this is where they'll be. *Woman, Home Alone, Meets with Unfortunate Demise.* Or gets mesothelioma from asbestos wrapping the pipes. Basements are places where, in horror movies, the monster awaits the unsuspecting, whether the monster is human or gaseous. Or else I'm afloat in Ultima Thule, adrift with sea creatures, beyond the borders of the known world. I carefully place my feet on each warped wood stair. At the bottom I stand before my parents' gray filing cabinet: the terror I'm currently confronting. I am checking to see whether it contains any of my old letters that I searched for elsewhere. I look here last because, when I open the drawers, some essence of my dead parents will surely escape.

The top drawer contains my parents' old tax returns, bank statements, car repair receipts, investment portfolios. They are as dingy and discolored as ancient explorers' maps that took them only so far. At some point cartographers simply left a blank space where the known world ended and the place where *"here be dragons and certain death"* began.

I do not find my old letters. In my memory the correspondence is written on onionskin and folded into delicate airmail envelopes—real letters conveying distance and loss more profoundly than email. I want to discover letters, notes, birthday cards to determine whether there were signs back then, as early as college, as early as high school, or even grade school that pointed toward or predicted my life's eventualities. I want to know firsthand who I once was as if that will tell me who I am today: an adolescent, a teenager, a girl, a woman—all rolled into one—terrified of dying.

Instead I discover a receipt from a long-ago plumbing repair project itemized in indecipherable handwriting. This aging sheet of numbers, from my parents' house in New Jersey, plunges me back to a day in tenth grade when I stared at a returned algebra exam, a red "D" on the top. Still, in my mind's eye, I know none of the equations make sense. The teacher's corrections also remain an incomprehensible set of facts.

Now that I think of it, I prefer not possessing so-called factual information. Maybe such a thing doesn't even exist. *Is anything factually true?* Really, my memory must be more all-knowing than a scrap of paper with inscrutable, enigmatic notations.

I open the second cabinet drawer. Startled, I discover the blood-stained Nazi flag that my ex-husband inherited from his father. It's a trophy from World War II, captured by this father who fought in the Battle of Normandy.

My ex left the flag behind, inadvertently. Apparently he didn't look here in the filing cabinet when he moved out.

I think of Pandora releasing evil upon the world by opening her famous box. A bit melodramatic, perhaps, but there's at least one way I'm like poor Pandora: Now that I've opened the drawer there's no going back.

From the way the flag is folded, the swastika seems to be only alternating stripes on a dirty white background. The rust-colored splotch could be any stain, not necessarily German (American?) blood. I'll let my ex know I found it since it means something to him. To me it's only a hex on my house.

I look around the basement for other monsters.

What does stuff mean, anyway? Will strangers, one day, peel through the physical remains of my life during some future estate sale? I imagine my things strewn across West Michigan. Or if no one wants my possessions perhaps all will replenish a landfill.

Again I consider mummification—sealed in a pyramid surrounded by a lifetime of furniture, knickknacks, my favorite polka-dot dresses, pink shoes and socks.

These embodiments of memory are often the smallest, most seemingly insignificant things. For example: inherited opera gloves, clutch purses, a roll of expired Lifesavers.

I discover eight pairs of my mother's opera gloves—leather, cloth, suede—tucked beneath a quilt in her antique trunk. They smell of Bellodgia. No they smell like mothballs. But I *want* to inhale carnation, jasmine, lily of the valley, the way they once smelled. I imagine my mother drifting into a ballroom, removing a chiffon scarf from wind-blown hair after arriving in a convertible. Benny Goodman plays a licorice stick of a clarinet, the big band swinging, Frank Sinatra crooning. Women twirl in satin and piqué, high-heeled mules to match, diamond earrings, delicate watches clasped beneath gloved wrists. Husbands wear tuxedos with ruby studs and patent leather dancing shoes. Couples sway across a black-and-white-movie dance floor.

I discover my mother's clutch purses in the wooden trunk as well. Black beads. Pearly beads. Red satin. I unclasp a stained white-satin clutch and find a thin tortoise-shell comb and a decades-old Kleenex. Do I feel my mother's fingerprints when I touch it? Is it possible for her prints to linger after she dies? Her things remained shadowed so long that they themselves are shadows, and mute, at least until now when I open them. Revive them.

When I think of relatives' houses, my fingers touch cotton chenille and flour-sack dishtowels. The soles of my feet tread tufted rugs. My grandmother's cheeks smelled of Vinolia soap with cold cream. Aunts offered jelly mints, Walnettos, Black Jack licorice chews, and Allsorts. In sixth grade I dabbed my mother's Evening in Paris perfume behind my ears. As a teenager I dabbed Wind Song and Canoe around the hems of my miniskirts.

The scent of English Leather . . . I am dancing with Jamie to "Blue Moon" across the wood floor of a gym in Glen Rock decorated to resemble Olde New York City.

So when I open boxed gloves and purses, the past breathes out. Memory *is* tangible, its folds creasing together like origami, awaiting a moment to be peeled open revealing a secret interior. Once memory splits open, I see that it's larger than mere fact, more perfect in its ability to embody sensory truth and metaphor. I give memories structure, resurrect them, like a new life-form, examine them anew.

This is what I *now* believe about my mother: When we lived in the West Indies, she was an artist. She stopped painting watercolors only because she lost her imagination once we moved to New Jersey, once confined to suburbia. She lost her direction, her nerve, her vision. She became like other housewives: vacuuming rugs, dusting, cooking dinner. Life became rote. She dropped anchor, refusing to sail into the unknown.

Sorting my parents' clothes after they die, I also find an unopened roll of Lifesavers in my father's jacket pocket. I sit on the carpet in their apartment holding it as if it contains a secret message. Lifesavers! I tuck them into my suitcase to bring home with me, where I then live, in Georgia.

My husband, soon after, secures a new teaching position in Michigan. "If we move, my parents won't be able to find me," I say to him.

"They're dead," he wisely points out.

Again I pack the roll of Lifesavers. I believe their ghosts will follow the sugary scent from Georgia to Michigan to the filing cabinet in the basement.

Of course I'm *relieved* my parents are dead. Who needs (yet another) set of bad, bad parents loose in the world? But maybe their ghosts will have learned the lessons of the past, will be more colorful, sweeter, rounder, with space in the middle to fill up with new selves. Perhaps their ghosts, able to taste the flavors of existence, will nourish themselves on cobwebs. Maybe *they* figured out how to survive death!

My Guardian Devils looking over me.

But, when you think about it, what's the point of possessing stuff since memory exceeds tangible things? Memory doesn't collect dust. It doesn't need to be placed in a moving van when you change locations. It doesn't even need an address on a map, since you carry it in your head at all times—always available, at the ready.

Still, to reach my parents' old filing cabinet, I must confront a monster of my own making: a collection of cardboard boxes saved after I moved here. Some boxes are flattened, most not. They are musty and mildewed, a moldy health hazard. Yet I'm unable to part with them. I will need them if I ever move again. Or pack up my hyperthymestic— obsessed-with-the-past—memories and ship them to the great beyond. Or pack up the love I feel for my sister, but am unable to tell her, and mail it to her, instead.

With my love of things I am about one teaspoon collection away from being a hoarder—as evidenced by my mound of useless boxes. Emotionally, spiritually, linguistically, I *am* a hoarder. I am the vessel, the vault, the basement, the cardboard boxes, the filing cabinet. I am the cobwebs. I am the dust. I am the roses yanked from the ground. I'm an ancient dictionary, an out-of-date atlas, and recent history. I am all the things that can't be abandoned because loss equals death. I have lost enough; therefore, I have already died enough.

This is the kingdom I have established to outlast death.
And all the creatures know it.

THE THREE FATES

When You Go

Your bathmat dries.

Snow drifts from the sky filling empty shoe prints.

Memories are frayed lace.

Love singes in August.

Sugar hardens. Flour writhes with weevils.

The mail that arrives through the door slot—circulars, postcards, pleas
   for your support—piles up, unforwardable.

OF CHRYSANTHEMUMS, TUPPERWARE, CREMATED REMAINS, AND FEDEX-ING TO THE GREAT BEYOND

exipotic: purgative; cleansing the body of illness

For example: "Can a tincture of dogs, of cats, of flowers, of dragons, of inherited treasures, of *stuff,* be exipotic? Or is memory a more reliable antidote?"

At dawn I watch out the window of my sister's house in Maine as her back disappears from sight. My last glimpse is of her short curly hair, bouncing, as she sprints past a street lamp. She jogs two hours a day. And even though she invited me to visit, I see little of her. Between her job and jogging, I spend much time alone. But not totally alone. For her Alaskan Malamute, Koya, keeps me company. Koya and I snuggle under a blanket on her couch. My sister's house is cold, the thermostat low, whereas I like a warm and toasty home. I shiver and wrap my hands under Koya's furry stomach. She nudges her head against my neck. I press my face against her, inhaling her wild, comforting scent.

My sister returns, sweating. Koya and I sit up expectant, welcoming.

"Got to shower and get ready for work," my sister says. She bounds up the staircase. Koya and I return to our dreams.

Later that evening, while my sister fixes dinner, Koya and I keep her company in the kitchen. In the middle of chopping vegetables, I pause to toss a slice of carrot up in the air for Koya. She leaps, snapping it in her mouth. No chewing. She swallows it whole, immediately. I repeat, repeat, repeat the process. I should finish the salad, but I prefer playing with Koya, who has perfect eye-mouth coordination. I toss each carrot slice a bit higher. She never misses.

After the game ends, I sit on the floor. Koya lies beside me, her head on my leg. She glances up at me, her eyes blue, cool, gentle. But it is my sister at the kitchen counter, her back to Koya and me, whom I want to look at me, see me. I don't know how to ask. She and I, now thirty-some years into our sisterhood, still cling to the absence, the distance of each other. It's as if we remain sitting on opposite sides on the back seat of our parents' car. We can't bridge the divide. Koya's presence, and *her* love, are surer.

Or were.

A year or so later my sister calls: Koya's dead. No real reason. My sister cries. Her grief is unexpected. I never heard her cry over childhood abandonments or the loss of our grandparents. I want to comfort her but worry I don't know how; if I say the wrong thing, she'll return to her distant self.

My sister plans to cremate Koya and keep the remains in her house.

For once I am in agreement with my sister. I keep the cremated remains of my cat, Quizzle, in a black plastic tin painted with red flowers on a bookcase in my office. A silk carnation, a miniature statue of an Egyptian cat, and a ceramic hummingbird adorn the small shrine.

Officially her name is spelled Qzl. A cat with no vowels. She didn't—or doesn't—need vowels. This magical cat contained all the stars and planets. She smelled of the moon and the sun, of the moisture of a suddenly ripe plum. Her deep green eyes reflected other centuries.

What will happen to her cremated remains when/if I die? Can she be buried with me? If I sail on *Pharoh's Fury* into an Afterlife can she accompany me?

I stare at Quizzle's photograph. She never leaves me. I can never leave her—that crystallization of the universe embedded in a feather of fur, in the breeze of a whisker soft as a petal.

Our mother dies a few years later, after Koya. This is when I fly from Atlanta to meet up with my sister in Rochester, Minnesota, where our parents retired. She and I oversee our mother's cremation and visit our father, suffering dementia. Sitting in the funeral parlor, awaiting the director, my sister says, "I'll keep the ashes."

I nod, relieved, as I certainly don't want my mother's ashes in my house, this constant reminder of death. Quizzle, an affirmation of life, is the only exception. My sister tells me her dog's ashes are in the sideboard in her dining room. She'll set Mom beside Koya.

"The *dining* room?" I say.

"What's wrong with that?" she asks.

Our father dies six days after my mother. My sister's too busy at work to make another trip. My husband and I fly to Rochester to oversee his cremation before driving my parents' Toyota, which I inherit, back home. What I haven't anticipated are my father's ashes, now locked in the trunk of the car.

"Guess it's safe to leave his ashes there." I nod toward the trunk. "Overnight." We stand in the parking lot of a Holiday Inn.

My husband looks at me as if I'm crazy.

Upon returning to Georgia, I bring my father to the FedEx office to mail him to Maine. My sister agreed to store his ashes, too. I fill out a form listing the contents of the package. I write "misc."

The bored clerk surveys the form. "You want extra insurance?" she asks.

"No," I say, and hand her my credit card.

I return alone to Rochester to clean out my parents' apartment. Among the papers and artifacts, I discover a brochure for Kikka-So, the Chrysanthemum Pavilion, of the Fujiya Hotel at Miyanoshita, Japan. Tucked inside the yellowing paper is a photograph of my father with four other white men seated at a table. A Japanese man (the owner?) hovers behind them.

After World War II my father, through his position as Chief Counsel of Trust Territories in the Interior Department, visited what was then known as "Occupied Japan." He traveled with a contingent of government officials in order to bring Japan back into the World Community.

The brochure explains:

Upon entering the Pavilion, one is struck with the simplicity. There are two kinds of sliding doors; Shoji (partition) and Kara-kami (Chinese-paper). They are necessary [because] carbon dioxide generated from charcoals burned in the Hibachi, the only heater in a Japanese house, would be harmful, or even dangerous, in a glass-closed room.

I wonder if the brochure was printed before the war. Postwar, post-bomb, would anyone worry about such minor forms of death?

I inherit an elegant raspberry-colored Japanese tea set from my parents. The words "Made in Occupied Japan" are stamped in gold leaf on the bottom. It adorns the mantel in my living room along with a porcelain saké set with gold-leaf decoration, likewise from Occupied Japan. A geisha's image is imprinted on the bottom of each cup. As you sip the rice wine you stare at slightly seductive porcelain features, a thin hint of a smile. These cups are older than I am. My first thought is that all the men who pressed their lips against this delicate china are dead, while the images of these women—who surely get the last smile—will survive forever.

We live in a white-frame house in DC, back when I'm a toddler, when my father traveled overseas. I'm surrounded by white: the dome of the Capitol, granite and marble memorials, monuments, all the white almost blinding me, until my very eyes seem to lack pigment. The air smells like cool slivers of moonlight.

The only true color in our house originates from my father's travels. We receive envelopes stamped with crimson pagodas, kings with golden crowns, foreign alphabets. We receive postcards featuring Alaskan totems, Hawaiian leis, trees swollen with Puerto Rican bananas, St. Croix sugarcane. My father brings me Siamese dolls and hula skirts. Only when letters slip through the slot in our white door, or when my father returns home with presents wrapped in pink tissue, is the air drenched mimosa, sandalwood, the heart of a lotus.

Once, I don a papier-mâché mask of a dragon stamped "Bangkok." I look at myself in the mirror and observe my little-girl body in my everyday dress. At the same time, I see a raspberry-pink face with black paint circling the eyes, lips puffy as bubblegum, whiskers curling across the cheeks. In the blink of an ornamental eye, I feel a green pendulous tail while four clawed toes evolve on each foot. I cradle a black pearl in my mouth and chew roasted swallows for dinner. My snout smells yellow jasmine. My carp scales sense a blue breeze from a pandanus fan. The world before me is the color of kumquats that I, as a dragon, tear open, to indulge my insatiable need for a life filled with an immortally indelible color.

I discover a second brochure from Japan while sorting through my parents' possessions. It describes the Cha-No-Yu, or tea ceremony, held at the Fujiya Hotel, with a rendering of a ceremonial tea gong on the cover. Cha-No-Yo is based upon the "adoration of beauty in the everyday routine of life. The rules governing the art and etiquette of it were formulated about 1500 A.D. and have been observed up to the present day without any substantial changes."

The sixteen-petaled chrysanthemum, a variety called "Ichimonjig-inu," is the flower of the imperial crest of Japan. It's honored on National Chrysanthemum Day called the "Festival of Happiness." According to the National Chrysanthemum Society, an ancient philosopher states:

"If you would be happy for a lifetime, grow Chrysanthemum." The chrysanthemum offers the power of a happy life. Less impressive, but still helpful, is that the boiled roots were once used to cure headaches.

Reading the brochure I enter the scent of chrysanthemums, Kure-bamboo, shady garden paths, cherry-blossom incense, koicha and usucha tea, and red camellias—gifts from Eastern gods, princes, and emperors.

I want to discover an escape hatch, a secret doorway, in order to slip from *this* life and enter the potent life of chrysanthemums. Just as I once entered the life of dragons, mystical creatures that never die.

Yet how happy or mystical was my father's life? He was a bad man who ended up in a black metal box in the trunk of his own Toyota driven by my husband and me to our home in Georgia. A funeral procession of sorts.

Now I wonder whether it would have been more practical, less expensive, and more fitting to dump his ashes, along with my mother's, into a green plastic container and call it a day.

Isn't Tupperware, which I bought at a party a few years ago, the perfect urn?

Existentially speaking, isn't Tupperware an incredibly useless/useful indestructible object?

I, however, do not, on any account, want to attend my one and only Tupperware party. But as a newly minted academic wife at a small college in Georgia, with otherwise no real existence or identity of my own, my husband strongly suggests that, if we want to fit in, I should go.

So here I am at the party, the only one not wearing pantyhose, heels, a color-coordinated outfit. I arrive in jeans, T-shirt, pink Reeboks, my hair yanked back in a ponytail. To seduce us into purchasing Tupperware, we are given little plastic presents, items to be tossed in a junk drawer. One is a red tweezer gadget that plucks stems off strawberries. Maybe it's practical but so are thumbs.

What most clearly stays with me from the party is one overheard conversation: A woman, talking to a friend, says she never dwells on the past. Apparently her mother died when she was young, but she refuses to think about it. *Why bother,* she says. *What good would it do? What's done is done.*

I rise up from my chair, tapping a spoon against my iced-tea glass for attention. *I have an announcement,* I say. *Remember everything. Forgetting is a form of death.* I point to the willfully forgetful woman. *Dwell upon, and remember, your mother whose death affects your present life. Even when you think you are putting it all behind you, you aren't.*

Store memories as if your skull is a filing cabinet, a canister, a jar, a vault, a repository, a Tupperware container containing all that happened.

The body embodies its whole story. Your story quivers on the breeze of your sighs.

View life through dark-tinted glasses.

But I do not deliver this sermon.

The words, stuck in my throat, cannot be tweezered out.

What I *wish* had happened at the party is as different from what actually happened . . . as the Tupperware party itself is as different from the tea ceremony described in the Japanese brochure:

> The room is fragrant with the smell of incense, awakening fond memories. While the guests are remarking that they have completely forgotten the cares of *this world* [emphasis mine, since surely there are other worlds], the curfew bells reach their ears.

Curfew bells. We all need bells, warnings, sounds of vigilance, to be on guard watching for, waiting for signs of incoming missiles, hydrogen bombs, all forms of impending doom.

I never discard the Tupperware even though it remains unused in my kitchen. No surprise since, as you recall, I flunked home economics. But maybe one day, when *I* hear the curfew bell, what remains of me might fit perfectly inside the green airtight container I reluctantly bought. My own eventual leave-taking done equally reluctantly—if not more so.

"They're all together in the sideboard," my sister says, calling to confirm the FedEx receipt of our father. "In the dining room."

Just as I suspected. I imagine the three canisters side-by-side: Dad, Koya, Mom.

If I die before my sister, I wonder if I'll become part of her collection. The thought of being displayed like a Hummel Collectible—whether in a Tupperware container or not—would definitely be the only thing worse than death.

MISS ROUTE 17'S BLUE PERIOD

sea smoke: fog

For example: "Do I see the world
clearly or through sea smoke?"

I discover a dead octopus one Galveston morning after spending the night on the beach. Tentacles swirl in tides as if it's still alive. I pick up a stick of driftwood and poke it. Even dead it's scary, prehistoric. I prod it farther up the sand away from waves and sit beside it, curious, now that it can't embrace me with suction cups, can't blind me with a stream of ink. This morning, however, I *am* blinded: by a sheen of aluminum sun reflecting off the Gulf.

I arrived here yesterday in a silent splash of moonlight with a man who isn't my husband. The man disappeared somewhere between Venus and Jupiter—into an expanse of inky sky.

"To survive in the deep ocean, octopuses evolved a copper rather than iron-based blood called hemocyanin, which turns its blood blue. This copper base is more efficient at transporting oxygen than hemoglobin when water temperature is very low and not much oxygen is around."[1]

Back in first grade, when I lived in DC, I knew a boy born blue. He suffered from a congenital heart disease, a condition called cyanosis (from Greek, *kyanos,* meaning dark blue). His blood wasn't receiving enough oxygen, hence his blue hue.

Afternoons, the blue boy sat on the front stoop of his house, usually silent. He never played hopscotch or marbles or jump rope. His lips and nail beds were darker blue than his face or arms. I once asked if I could touch his lips. He nodded. I pressed a finger to them then looked to see if the blue transferred. It hadn't. I wanted to be blue, too. His skin was magical, unlike my own.

I colored my nails blue with a crayon. It didn't last.

Neighbors whispered that the blue boy would die young. And indeed one day he was there; one day he wasn't. Nevertheless, the indelibility of the blue boy himself remains with me. His magical blue remains *on* me.

My husband may or may not notice my absence this Galveston morning. Maybe he can't see me here by the Gulf as if camouflaged by ink. Maybe, while I slept, the octopus injected me with poison paralyzing me, confusing my sense of smell, taste, and sight. My sense of right and wrong.

I lie back on the sand, my long tangled hair heavy with mist. My damp skirt clings to my thighs. My sheer white blouse offers scant protection.

The jagged caw of seagulls unravels from a pale blue horizon. A tincture of night presses my tongue, a taste that lingers.

Penny with a Tail was my other mystical childhood friend in DC. Not that I knew for sure she had a tail. It was only a rumor circulating around the neighborhood. So I never saw it though I endlessly imagined it. I wanted to believe in it. Maybe these two magical children existed because we all lived across the street from a cemetery. Dead people living so close to me—not that you could say they actually lived—scared me. I knew the necessity of amulets in order not to get dragged beneath the earth where they, in whatever form, dwelled. When I walked across the cemetery, walked right on top of them, I felt lucky none thrust a desiccated hand out of the ground to grab my ankle.

Penny with the Tail and Blue Boy were, in effect, emissaries sent to protect me from death and otherworldly hazards. I, aglow in their aura, was safe.

Surely myths override reality, are more enduring. Under the spell of my friends, even after Blue Boy died, I was likewise anointed with a blue shawl of unending destiny.

I miss the rawness of an unsettled me, one I prefer to the *now* me who knows better than to spend the night on a beach with a stranger . . . a "me" who has forgotten how to take risks. I long for that morning on the Galveston beach because the ache deposits me back to a time of possibilities. I realize the options were negative ones. But maybe I can long for that younger version of me without needing to *be* her.

How can I long for a past full of regret?

To live you have to be wounded.

Years after that day in Galveston, I am channel surfing and see the man, that stranger, starring in a movie. Later I see him in another movie. He is tall and blonde. Perfect. How did we find each other on a beach in Galveston? He would not remember me, I'm quite sure. I am the only one who remembers. And, because I do, in that moment I see a life of what might have been.

An octopus's arms contain neurons separate from its brain, with its own set of memories, knowing how, say, to open a shellfish, while its eyes glance around for danger, death, sex, blue octopus love.

I want to touch the octopus even though it scares me. I turn on my side until my eye is a few inches from a tentacle. I briefly swipe a finger across it. Sticky. Squishy. It smells of ancient underwater caves. I imagine diving deep into fathomless water that tinges my skin transparent blue, yet also opaque enough to hide me, sprouting blue limbs to propel me away.

Dusk is electric blue or rose-blue or limestone blue or pearl blue or inky blue or the moment in late afternoon when love, death, loss, and longing, all together, halo the day moon. Everything feels close to me clinging like sand on moist skin.

I could live in an underwater cave where dusk casts blue shadows across muddy sand. I could live alone with only blue memories grasping me like tentacles of an octopus.

That night, still in the white skirt and blouse, I sit in a Galveston bar troubled with tanned men cradling bottles of Shiner or shots of cheap anything. Sea smoke obscures lights mirroring the bar, blueing them. I am the girl perched on the last stool at a quarter past midnight dreaming my way toward morning, deep with blue regret that I wear forever.

I do not think any of these thoughts in the moment. Only later, now, am I nostalgic for that encounter on the beach with the man and the dead octopus—for all past moments, even if painful. I remember each period of time as a brilliant wash of color regardless of loss, abandonment, death: blue and timeless as metaphor. Memory isn't a transcription of what happened. Memory is emotional history. A language of the senses. Memory colors outside the lines turning, in this case, everything blue.

Before I run out of oxygen, before my skin turns blue, I need to tell these stories about a blue boy, about a girl with a tail, about an octopus—stories to decipher how to understand love—which is a way to understand death. Loss of love being itself a kind of death.

So even though I have been *mis*-loved *and* have been unloving—even though the ache has been smoky, deep, and blue—I wish I had three hearts like an octopus: three times the longing, three times the regret. But also three times the love, three times the life.

THE THREE FATES

Filling in the Blanks

To ease our minds, we clip coupons for baby powder, toothpaste, paper products. Canned food for our pet boa constrictor. An ant farm. We embroider comforting homilies to decorate our walls: "We're born into this world crying, and we leave it vainly gasping for air," sayeth Schopenhauer.

Upon your arrival, we distribute crossword puzzles. You will believe that if you answer all the questions correctly, if you know the word for six across, a reprieve will be granted. No reprieve will be granted. It is merely to fill in— not words—but poor attempts to reweave frayed tapestries once rich with silver horses, twilight, and fate. But the tapestries are now distributed to lost clouds about which you once dreamed.

Twenty-three across: It makes no difference.

Nothing makes any difference. All the lions' beards are tangled. All the dots on dominoes fade. The scent of a city in summer hardens. Thoughts are truncated in the middle of a line. No, no, nothing.

The blanks will always spell "adjourned," as prescribed by *Death's Rules of Order*.

Caskets line the horizon like oil freighters heading out to sea.

We watch *Wheel of Fortune*. We, just like you, hope for grand prizes, free cruises. Washers and dryers. Subscriptions for life.

ON THE RELIANCE OF VERBS
TO SURVIVE DEATH

chronesthesia: the brain's ability to maintain
simultaneous awareness of past, present, and
future and to travel back and forth between them

I sit in a rental car in an office parking lot in Atlanta watching for a blue Pathfinder, the car my former therapist, Randy, drives. I glance at my watch. He's late. It's 10:15 a.m., Friday, May 13, 2005. I stopped seeing him regularly when I moved to Michigan several years ago. Maybe he drives another car now. I decide to wait in the lobby. I present myself to the receptionist who looks aghast, telling me Randy died two days ago. Heart attack. She wasn't expecting me since I'm no longer a regular client. She's so sorry.

She urges me into his private office to be alone, take my time.

I slump on the familiar blue couch, bereft.

He died here in his office Wednesday afternoon. It's not clear to me whether the ambulance arrived first or not.

I must morph three time frames together: the "me" who I was/am when I live(d) in Georgia, when I was/am still his regular patient; the "me" who I was/am sitting on the couch two days after his death; and the "I" who I am *now,* at 2:34 p.m., May 13, 2015, in my home in Michigan. My responsibility here, as I discover how to survive death, is to merge selves and time frames into one present continuous moment. I must re-create the past as if it's the present: all eras coalescing into *now.* I refuse to consider the death of any given day. I carry each day forward with me.

In his office, after learning of his death, I spy his eyeglasses and legal pad, a green ballpoint pen clipped to it. Coffee dregs remain in a Styrofoam cup, his Nike tennis shoes on the floor—for all time.

I place his glasses in my purse. A few minutes later I talk to a friend on my cell phone who convinces me I'm not thinking clearly. I shouldn't, in effect, steal Randy's glasses. His family might want them.

I return them to the cushion. I also decide against taking his Nikes. I unclip the plastic ballpoint pen from the pad of paper claiming it instead. On it is printed, will *always* be printed: *American Homecare Supply, Georgia.*

A secret message?

What I should not do, but do anyway, is glance at his legal pad to glean the last words he wrote. But his familiar handwriting is a jumble of names and phone numbers. They could be plumbers, electricians. Just ordinary notations of a seemingly ordinary day.

A placard hanging on the wall reads: "Barbie Is Anorexic." This is new, the first time I see it. I consider the clients he leaves behind.

On the end table is a seashell, my own pearl-pink West Indian conch, a going-away present I gave to him when I moved to Michigan. I put it in my bag as well.

I imagine Randy, a bachelor, leaving his condominium for work Wednesday morning. Dishes remain unwashed in his sink. Damp towels in his bathroom.

His dog Mocha awaited his return . . . *still awaits his return.*

I was so certain—*am* so certain—of his arrival this Friday morning, I review, while waiting in the car in the parking lot, the words I wanted—want—to tell him. That secret I've never told anyone: that night in New Jersey, the blood, the pink-tiled bathroom. Now, sitting on Randy's blue couch, I believe(d) I'll (I'd) never tell anyone. If not

Randy . . . Even though my therapy with Randy had formally ended, I plan(ned) to tell him today. I was/am finally ready.

The air-conditioning in his office is, as always, too cold. It always will be too cold. As if *he'll* always be here waiting for me to ask him to adjust the AC forevermore.

"For us convinced physicists, the past, present and future is an illusion, although a persistent one." Albert Einstein

I leave the rented car in the parking lot and aimlessly wander sidewalks past shops and cafés. The area is familiar: air scented by azaleas, pine straw, and the deepening humidity of a Southern spring. Except, on the other hand, nothing seems familiar. I've been gone from Georgia for years. I walk neighborhoods through a glare of heat. Sweat beads the nape of my neck beneath my long hair. I wander block after block looking for something. As if I'll find a "thing," an "essence" of Randy, *here or here or here.*

I pass a public library: newspapers, obituaries, funeral announcements. I enter and ask a librarian for copies of *The Atlanta-Journal Constitution* for the past few days.

Randy Groskind, 53, of Smyrna, died May 11, 2005. Mr. Groskind . . . was a therapist for several years with Metro Atlanta Psychological Services. . . . Graveside services will be Sunday, May 15, 2005 at 11:30 AM at Arlington Memorial Park. . . .

I've brought no appropriate clothes for a funeral. I enter a boutique and am dazed by colorful merchandise, the scent of new clothes more alive than I myself feel. Red, lavender, yellow blouses, skirts, dresses. Nothing suitable. A clerk asks if she can help. I shake my head. I can't speak, as if weeds clog my throat.

My skin: frozen in his office, sweaty out on the street, frozen in the air-conditioned library and boutique. Heat. Cold. Heat. Cold. It hardly matters. Both are numbing.

I stumble outside. Afternoon deepens. Sun sears oxygen, strands of breath, as if I no longer remember how to inhale.

On Sunday I stand graveside at Arlington Memorial Park surrounded by Randy's family, friends, coworkers. Heat. Cold. No breeze ripples the cemetery as if stilled by acres of dead bodies. Every rib in my chest feels frozen. A rabbi prays, words indistinguishable whether he speaks Hebrew or English. I wear a tan dress I bought in another shop. I never wear it again. For years it remains in my closet on a hanger—limp, formless—before I donate it to the Salvation Army.

The short ceremony ends. I am handed a shovel. I scoop bits of red clay onto Randy's coffin. I don't hear the thud against wood.

Driving away from the cemetery, I set Randy's pen on the seat beside me. I worry I might leave behind the Homecare, the *soul-care* he supplied me. How does the present-me tell the present-then me not to worry? Do you join the dead? Resurrect them? Re-create them through sound, memory, verb tense into the present?

James Baldwin says, for the "dead their days had ended and I did not know how I would get through mine."

While still in Michigan, before flying to Georgia, I receive an email from Randy on Wednesday afternoon only a couple of hours before he dies. I emailed him first, telling him I look forward to seeing him on Friday, but am nervous, too. I haven't seen him in a long time.

He writes, "I'm still here. Everything will be fine."

Night floats down onto the Atlanta airport. The red and white lights on planes seem bright, harsh. My image reflected in the window grays to translucence, as if I enter the glass, where I won't feel the absence of his presence. Or as if I am the ghost, not he.

Maybe I should have taken his eyeglasses. He is the first person to understand me, as if, with his glasses in my possession, he will see me forever.

I save his email: *I'm still here. Everything will be fine.* Years later everything is—and everything isn't.

I want to respond.

I do.

This is it.

THE QUEEN OF PANMNESIA

panmnesia: belief that all mental
impressions are stored in memory

Every Wednesday, after the hypnotist greets me, he walks behind me down the stairs to his office. But shouldn't I be following *him* down, down to where this guide to the subconscious leads me? He seeks to help me understand my fear of death.

I tell him I suffer from a form of limerence—in my case obsessive thoughts about death. And wanting death, somehow in return, to acknowledge my devotion. Or do I have chronic melancholia? Or maybe my diagnosis is existential pneumonia, a Dadaist flu, a condition from which one never recovers. Or maybe all along I experience hiraeth, a homesickness for a home to which I can never return, a home which maybe never was. Hiraeth is nostalgia, yearning, grief for lost places of my past, a never-ending word, a forever and ever feeling. The purity of a home that exists only in imagination.

Home. Many different kinds of home exist. I've never felt at home in my own body, my own skin. All my restless searching. Do I particularly fear death because I've never fully figured out—discovered—life?

The hypnotist no longer sees clients in the office with that waiting room. Here, two walls in his new office are stuffed with books on psychology, biofeedback, and hypnosis. Four low windows line another wall level with the ground. Outside the windows and across the road is Lake Michigan. African violets bloom on the window ledge. A vase of flowers decorates his desk.

I hear nothing this winter evening. The windows are dark. I am cocooned in this room as if stillness itself waits for me to unburden myself of secrets. I sit in a green easy chair. I switch off the lamp beside it. I prefer air the color of dusk. Of twilight. It's a quiet, well-ordered, subterranean habitat in which to enter the subconscious.

Hypnosis, in this case a form of meditation, will help ease scary thoughts, fears about all forms of death, images that inhabit my mind. Once I fully learn to meditate, I will better understand what happened in the past. Here I'll meander through all time knowing that I must, in particular, return to that pink-tiled bathroom in New Jersey, *that night, that night, that night,* no one knows about. The anxiety toward it, toward death, toward life, will lessen.

In this room I am ready. This room is quiet as a phrontistery, a thinking place.

"Find a spot on the ceiling," the hypnotist says. "Look up. Not with your head but with your eyes."

I stare at a knot in the pine ceiling.

"I'll count to three," he says. "Eyes already closing."

His voice is low as he urges me to enter a state of relaxation. My gaze remains fixed on the same spot until my eyelids grow heavy, fatigued. I breathe slowly, fully. When I exhale, tension releases from my diaphragm, rising up through my throat, out between my lips. The wood knot in the ceiling disappears behind my lids.

He tells me I will feel a warm sensation spread across my shoulders. Waves of warmth release tension. In this release, images focus. I'll see my life more clearly.

I am no longer in his office.

I am with my Scotch terrier on an autumn day in Vermont. The moment I hit him with his leash.

I am here to place memories, snippets of thought, my crimes and misdemeanors, on the floor in his office. Offerings. Petitions for forgiveness. I am here to whisper my transgressions, the dead-ends, the wrong turns. I will repeat and repent until all is transformed into another shape altogether. One that's clearer, one more resembling life than death.

The hypnotist tells me I first encountered a form of death, a spiritual death, with my father. All the other forms of death deepened and evolved from that.

Yes, but what about . . .

I tell the hypnotist about the doctor who drove the blue convertible, that lost weekend in the emergency room. After that weekend I imagined standing on the shore on Galveston Island. All I saw was a dry Gulf of Mexico. I was tugged by a mystical sea as if I would drown in an ocean of bones.

I wanted to drown even though I'm scared of dying.

I swallowed those pills even though I'm scared of dying.

But I didn't swallow enough pills. Perhaps I tempted death, tempted fate, simply to affirm I'm still alive.

In the pause between words, I slip out of one image and into another, slipping between words, between worlds, morphing past and present.

Death is tangible and intangible. Death is a heavy summer day when the sun turns jaundiced, mustard yellow. Death is the scent of red bricks in autumn or lilies in spring. Death is a feather that crests a breeze before fluttering to the ground. It is foam that curls a wave before ebbing from sight. Except it's also an obliteration of senses.

But the body itself doesn't disappear in death: It can be unearthed, touched, studied. Salvador Dalí, best known for his painting "The Persistence of Memory," was recently exhumed to perform a paternity test. His famous waxed moustache was, by all accounts, still perfectly curled.

The hypnotist loads a biofeedback program into his computer. He clips a sensor onto my ear lobe. Each time my heart beats, blood pulses into the tissue. The sensor projects my pulse rate onto the computer screen.

Irrationally, I believe my life itself will appear on the computer as if on a TV screen. I'm scared to see those images. I pull off the sensor.

I should be relieved to see tangible evidence of my pulse, my heart rate—evidence I'm still breathing—but it's too much. Too much that the body itself, its functions, can be measured, graphed on a computer.

The hypnotist urges me to clip the sensor back on my ear. Reluctantly I do. The lines are jagged. It's as if there are two of me: the "me" sitting in the chair; the "me" breathing on the screen. My breath is contrapuntal: two melody lines operating independently of each other.

I could be an octopus with a backup heart in case one fades to a distant throb on the ocean floor. The longer I continue to breathe, however, the breath of the "me" sitting in the chair appears more in sync with the lines on the computer.

I inhale. Pause. Exhale. Pause. The lines rise. Pause. Fall. Pause.

My heart that night under the boardwalk . . . I imagine a heart rate with gaps. That man pulls my arm.

Gap.

I stop breathing.

Gap

My heart stops beating.

Gap.

He pins my hair, my body to the sand. My heartbeat feels wiry, spinning away from my body.

He leaves no visible scars. Yet inside I feel bloodied, bones fragmented, an implosion of lungs. He hurts only one part of my body, but I ache everywhere. When I leave the boardwalk that night, I feel naked, pieces of my body disorganized. But no one sees that girl stumbling home.

Several months after that first biofeedback session, the hypnotist again says to fixate on a spot on the ceiling. He invites me to envision a staircase I've never imagined before, bringing me to a new place, a darker place, deeper into the psyche, deeper into my past. This staircase is stone. Chipped from bedrock. Lit by torches with a metal railing. He asks me to stand at the top and look down. Torches flicker all the way to the bottom.

"I'm going to count to twenty," he says. "With each count take another step. Twenty steps. Down, down, down, deep . . . deeper . . . One . . ."

As he says each number, I glide down steps, my feet protected by soft leather sandals. The trance moves up my ankles to my knees, my throat. The numbers the hypnotist speak sound distant. With each one I am more weightless. At the bottom of the staircase is a heavy wood door. My fingertips touch a metal knob. I open the door and there I am—a younger me—my hair in a ponytail, the way I wore it in high school.

I step into the room. I enter night. Red shadows. Something is tumbling. No, it's sliding.

He asks which room I'm in.

In the bathroom, but I don't know if I say this aloud.

I hear silence in his office. I hear loud colors in the bathroom.

I feel it, feel it . . . sliding out of me. I try to hold it . . . liquidy, clotting . . . I'm unable to grasp it . . .

It shreds like tissue. Like liquid tissue. Liquid tissue that clots.

He asks me what it is. I know what it is. I don't want to know what it is.

I try to save it. It. Her. I try to save *her.*

But there is nothing.

There is no one to save.

I've wanted to say good-bye. She has disappeared.

The Three Fates—Clotho, Lachesis, Atropos—visit a child three days after its birth to decide its life and its fate. But suppose a baby doesn't live three days? Not even three hours. Not three minutes. Or three seconds. Does that mean *I* held its fate in my own hands all along? *I* killed it? Her?

When I open the door I see blood on pink tiles on the bathroom floor.

Carnage: fluid and delicate.

I am a metaphor for darkness. Darkness is a metaphor for me.

During the next session, I tell the hypnotist what happened after the night at the bachelor party, the night with the prostitutes and the gun. I explain what happened after I returned home, all the pills I swallowed. That's the night when the Galveston "me" most clearly encountered the teenage "me."

For years, until today, now with the hypnotist, I feel as if I'm asleep and awake at the same time, unable to stop the insistent memory of a baby not yet a baby.

Therefore, dead.

I tell him.

I tell him about *her*.

New Jersey.

Her.

Did I kill it? Her? I tell him and tell him about that night in New Jersey. Pink tiles. Blood. Pink tiles. Blood.

"No, no," he says. "No, no," he repeats. "No. A miscarriage is. . ." I hear his explanation yet don't hear it. He is not holding me accountable. He says I am not responsible.

But it made me feel as if I'm transubstantiated into the dead baby— or the dead baby into me.

He says he doesn't think that's who I am. His voice remains quiet, slow, steady. He does not sound alarmed or horrified when I tell him about that night.

I remember that one day, about a year ago, when I had that sonogram: *Now*, I think, I watched that screen half-hoping, half-expecting to see her. She's been the one trying to send me a signal. A message. Maybe it was even *her* palm that touched my heart in that wide-awake dream. Her ghost, her soul, a snippet of a fingernail remain. I haven't lost everything. I haven't lost everything that once was her.

One mistake. One wrong step off the boardwalk. One wrong night. One wrong man. One wrong girl. And my womb unmoors an ocean of death draining nowhere and forever.

The knife-thin man did not kill me. Only her.

After he left I must have pulled on my clothes. I must have walked back to the cottage. I must have sat in the bathtub. The water must have been steaming. I wonder if I singed her although she couldn't yet have been a "her."

The word "pain" from Latin means "fine, penalty." There is a penalty when you're not inoculated against pain. The pain was/is/always will be slow. A slow pain penalizing life.

If the girl had been born what would her eyes have looked like when she cried? When I told her about the man, the boardwalk, the moment I turned in the wrong direction. The girl's eyes would be the color of mercy.

I dream about sliding a pair of tiny wool mittens on her hands. Except I always forget to purchase them. Her hands are cold-blue even in summer.

After that night, the inside of my skin is cold-blue all summer. I lie on a towel on the grass in my backyard in Glen Rock. The sun splashes me with particles of night. The inside of my stomach feels distended with loss. I believe I look pregnant.

As I talk I feel *it* again. *Her* again. As if she is pushing, pushing, pushing to depart my body. But I know there will be no "she." All that will erupt onto the floor of the hypnotist's clean carpet is a sponge-like ooze of memory. *Her* death. My body re-creates that moment as if expecting a different outcome. My body will discover a different history.

I feel memory-blood pool around my feet. I tried to kill myself so I could find her.

"Would you have found her?" he asks.

I shake my head, no, my eyes closed.

But maybe, maybe, maybe . . . my thoughts stall, utterly. No, they can't stall. They drift downward even further to a damp punishing thought I've never heard before: Maybe part of me wanted her to die . . .

Open your eyes.

I am asleep. I am awake. Still I sit in the chair in his office. There is no baby. No blood. *Where is it?* I ask.

It feels as if it happened yesterday. No, today. Ten minutes ago. It feels as if it will happen tomorrow.

"You can let it go now," he says.

Let all of it go?

I have to tell him: "Suppose part of me wanted her to die?"

"That feeling would be normal." Again he reassures me. Normal . . . that I'd be as scared to give birth to her as I was to lose her.

I both did and didn't give birth to a Girl with No Name. A girl with no mouth, no eyes, no ears, no nose, no fingers. No veins. No heart. No mind.

The archaic word for one who absolves is "absolvant."

The archaic word to heal is "sanative."

"Do you feel different?" the hypnotist asks the next time I see him.

"I always thought my body killed her."

He tells me that sometimes our bodies aren't ready to sustain something as delicate as life. But that isn't the same as killing it. "Your body simply wasn't ready," he says.

I wasn't ready. My mind wasn't ready.

I explain how everything inside my body felt as if it drained right out of me. She has no narrative. No story. No past, present, or future.

What I hear, *what I think he says*, is "she's a latent seed." I repeat what I think he has said.

"I said latency," he explains. "Not latent seed."

We both smile at the misunderstanding. Both are true.

A latency: a time interval, a time delay between cause and effect. In that interval she slipped away, disappearing.

Latent seed: a state of existing but not yet developed.

I was scared of death, of dying, *before* that night in the pink-tiled bathroom. *Way* before. And maybe I was scared I killed her in a different—yet still definitive—way that my father killed me. All my previous fears around death, as well as the subsequent ones, simply coalesced around that night. Associations, memories pile atop one another. I, an archaeologist, sort through the rubble.

We—*I*—can't always know or pinpoint the exact origins of a state of being like a location on a map. Maybe the origin of my fear of death was embedded in me during my own birth as if this sliver of life—mine—was born able to foretell my future.

Or maybe the girl I've always missed—or grieved—is the paper-doll girl ripped in the ruin of childhood. Maybe these two girls became inseparable, interchangeable. Maybe the miscarried girl simply compounded the loss.

I explain this to the hypnotist. He nods. "The miscarried girl reminded you of the 'real girl,'" he agrees.

The "real" me, ripped in another way, by my father.

Abandoned.

Abandonment: The word I used in the imagined letter to Jeffrey Dahmer. Aren't all abandonments forms of death? If I've always feared, yet encountered, abandonment, then of course I'm terrified of death. Death is the ultimate abandonment. Abandonment of self.

A young woman ahead of me in the grocery checkout line wears gray sweats, slightly dirty, and scuffed sneakers. Even though she is young, her back hunches as if she is old, exhausted. She places a single item on the counter: a pregnancy kit.

I worry this is potentially bad news. She wears no wedding ring, but, more than that, I sense she is exhausted because she is scared.

The cashier runs the kit across the scanner. The young woman asks where the restroom is. The cashier points just past the check-out line. She opens her wallet and hands the cashier a few rumpled dollar bills.

As if trudging through snow, the woman walks toward the ladies room. The cashier and I stare at each other, no doubt thinking the same thing. "Maybe I should see if she's okay," I say.

I push open the door to the ladies room. Three stalls, only one occupied. I see her scuffed sneakers below the door. "Sweetie," I say, "Are you okay?"

"Are you the woman behind me in line?" she asks from behind the closed stall.

"Yes," I say.

She explains that the test results are inconclusive. The wand doesn't show her to be pregnant or not. "I think I did it wrong," she says.

She hands me the box from under the closed door so I can read the directions.

"I drank some water earlier," she says, "but I don't think I had enough pee to get a result."

I look inside the box. "There's a second wand in here," I say. "Maybe drink more water, wait a bit. Try again."

The woman opens the door to the stall. "I *can't* be pregnant."

I tell her I hope she isn't.

"Do you have kids," she asks me.

Yes.

But I shake my head: *No. I don't.*

I want to bring the woman home with me. I want to be with her when she discovers the test results. I want to feed her. I want her to be all right.

"Thanks," she says. I hand her the box with the remaining wand. She tells me she'll go home and drink more water.

I watch as she opens the door, watch her, until the door closes.

The following Wednesday I tell the hypnotist about the woman in the grocery store. I tell him I wish I'd gotten her name and phone number.

I want to know how she got pregnant. Suppose . . .

Suppose she's like me. Suppose the same thing that happened to me happened to her.

The first time I saw the hypnotist, on October 31, it's shortly before the presidential election between Barack Obama and Mitt Romney. During that first session, I tell the hypnotist I'm scared Romney might win, that we'll regress to a nonempathetic wealthy white man as president. Four years later I am crushed when Donald Trump becomes president, that Hillary Rodham Clinton won't be our first woman president. I can't get out of bed the day after the election. My body feels weighted with fear, anxiety, despair, sadness.

Over the months fear increases. I feel as if the man under the boardwalk, the man in the blue convertible, the Poet, my father, all these men inhabit Donald Trump's psyche . . . *are* his psyche. They are all one and the same.

For the first time in the hypnotist's office I say the word "rape." I say that this man we now call "president" is, by many accounts, a sexual predator. As are many other men. I think about, worry about, the woman who bought the pregnancy test and how she might have gotten pregnant.

I think of my aunt murdered in her antiques store. My friend Joanne, murdered in her apartment in New York City, has now been dead for decades. I wonder what scared the lonely women once sequestered in McLean Gardens. Maybe they were right to be scared.

All the women.

One day after the inauguration of Donald Trump I stroll the streets of Grand Haven wearing my point-eared, pink-knit "pussy" cap in protest—a one-woman Women's March.[1] No one I pass comments on my cap. Though I walk alone, I know I'm not alone.

Of course I'm not alone. I feel the energy of the hundreds of thousands of women across the country, also in pink caps, also marching, also resisting. We are more powerful because of each other—our voices stronger.

Then, months later, during the week of October 16, 2017, more than twelve million #MeToo posts appear during the first twenty-four hours. Mine is one of them: *Men sexually assaulted me, too.* The guilty are being called to account, even if not all of them can be *held* to account. By others. By me.

I first saw the hypnotist after sitting in his waiting room in his old office. Now I've entered a room beyond a waiting room, entered a story whereby I choose the ending, choose to end wherever and however I want. If not *when*ever I want.

Even if I die (I'm still holding out for *if!*), I've finally gathered together all my various selves—words and memories—which comprise the past. So this is my confession, my testament, because, if I have to go, I'm not going quietly.

The past is at once perpetual and ephemeral, says Jonah Lehrer Proust.

"I hate for anything to end," I say to the hypnotist.
"What does that mean to you?" he asks.
"Abandonment."
He nods. "Sadly, life contains so much of it."
"It all resembles death," I say.
"Yet you've survived. You're still here." He almost smiles. "And living is more about integration," he adds. "It's about constructing a narrative." The hypnotist says that another form of survival is to live life fully in the face of abandonment *and* death.

He retrieves a book from his shelf and reads a quote from the developmental psychoanalyst Erik Erikson. "'I am what survives of me,'" he says. "'That's true, too.'"

I am what survives of me. I type this sentence on January 24, 2018, at 2:45 p.m. How else to make sense of the past, of life, of *my* life, except by processing it with words? I consider the paradisiacal sun in my uncle's apartment when we tapped our way through summer days. Did my uncle stop typing when he ran out of words, jokes, or heart? Or simply out of time? But his jokes, his words remain.

I want to keep Qwertying, living, immortalizing this moment. And the next. As each becomes a memory, I keep writing *as if,* with one more word, maybe I *will* obtain the unobtainable.

I sojourned from page 180 in *Hammond's Contemporary World Atlas,* Washington DC, where I was born, to here, to page 186, to this hypnotist in Grand Haven, Michigan. Seemingly only six pages but, on the circuitous route, I traveled backward and forward. I drove, flew, meandered, ruminated, meditated, and survived.

So now I beg of The Fates a dispensation in order to pursue endless new peregrinations. If they refuse, then I pray the length of my string be long, and when it's finally cut *I will* live on in others—in the heaven of their memories, in the wake of these words.

Acknowledgments

A profound thanks to Alicia Christensen, Emily Wendell, Anna Weir, Joeth Zucco, Rosemary Sekora, Courtney Ochsner, Patty Beutler, and everyone at the University of Nebraska Press for their continued support of my writing. I am deeply, and always, grateful.

Some sections in this book were previously published (in different forms and sometimes with different titles) in the following journals or anthologies:

"On the Reliance of Verbs to Survive Death" (published under the title "The Ten Year Wake"), brevity.com.

"The Safe Side," *Blue Mesa Review*, winner of the 2015 essay contest.

"Until My Number Comes Up" (published as "Until My Number Is Up"), *Creative Nonfiction*, placed second in the themed issue on "Waiting."

"Requiem for a Qwertyist" (published as "The Qwertyist"), *From Curlers to Chainsaws: Women and Their Machines*, edited by Joyce Dyer, Jennifer Cognard-Black, and Elizabeth MacLeod Wells (Michigan State University Press, 2016).

"Miss Route 17 Refuses to Grow Old" (published as "A Whole Lotta [Middle-Aged] Love"), *The Rumpus*.

"Death Comes for the Poet," *Superstition Review*.

"13 Ways of Resurrecting New Jersey," Section 4, (published as "Cupcake Days"), *Writerlicious: Anthology on Food,* edited by Kim Aubrey (Red Claw Press, 2011).

Notes

MISS ROUTE 17 REFUSES TO GROW OLD

1. Adam Bert, "Adam Shines!," *Adam Bert Daily*, (blog) July 19, 2010, https://adamquotedaily.wordpress.com/2010/07/19/adam-shines-in-cherry-photoshoot/.

2. "Adam Lambert Says 'Keep Speculating About His Sexuality,'" MTV, May 28, 2009 http://www.mtv.com/news/1612269/adam-lambert-says-keep-speculating-about-his-sexuality/.

3. ItsGina's, "Adam Lambert Behind the Music Documentary," YouTube, May 17, 2016 https://www.youtube.com/watch?v=_7cMLpQEL7w.

4. ItsGina's, "Adam Lambert Behind the Music Documentary," YouTube.

5. "Jean de Jandun on Parisian Gothic Buildings," Oberlin College, accessed October 1, 2018, http://www2.oberlin.edu/imagesArt336/jandun.html.

THE SICK HYPOCHONDRIAC

1. "Oil of the Five Thieves," Snerious Press, January 19, 2015, http://snerious.com/blog/oil-of-the-five-thieves/.

MY LIFE AS A THANATOLOGIST

1. Catharine Arnold, *Necropolis: London and its Dead,* (London: Simon & Schuster UK, 2008), 5-6. Kindle.

2. Arnold, *Necropolis,* 20.

3. "Sedlec Ossuary 'Bone Church'" Atlas Obscura, accessed October 16, 2018, https://www.atlasobscura.com/places/sedlec-ossuary.

4. Matthew Gunther, "Why I Mummified a Taxi Driver," *Chemistry World,* February 22, 2017, https://www.chemistryworld.com/careers/why-i-mummified-a-taxi-driver/2500178.article.

5. "More Fun with Jeremy Bentham," *Lowering the Bar,* June 4, 2013, https://loweringthebar.net/2013/06/more-fun-with-Jeremy Bentham.html.

6. Rose Troup Buchan, "Chinese theme park sets up 'death simulator' where volunteers can experience being cremated," *Independent*, May 5, 2015, https://www.independent.co.uk/news/world/asia/chinese-theme-park -sets-up-death-simulator-where-volunteers-can-experience-being-cremated -10226314.html.

THE JANET LEIGH VARIATIONS

1. McLean Gardens (website), accessed September 20, 2018, http://www .mcleangardents.com/home.asp.

MISS ROUTE 17'S BLUE PERIOD

1. Rachel Newer, "Ten Curious Facts About Octopuses," Smithsonian.com, October 31, 2013, https://www.smithsonianmag.com/science-nature/ten -curious-facts-about-octopuses-7625828/.

THE QUEEN OF PANMNESIA

1. "Donald Trump's comments about women and 'grabbing them by the pussy' have spurred many women into action and led to the creation of hand-knitted pink pussy hats which thousands of demonstrators are expected to turn up in." Fiona Keating, *International Business Times*, January 14 (updated January 18), 2017.

The Distance Between:
A Memoir
Timothy J. Hillegonds

Opa Nobody
by Sonya Huber

Pain Woman Takes Your
Keys, and Other Essays
from a Nervous System
by Sonya Huber

Hannah and the Mountain:
Notes toward a Wilderness
Fatherhood
by Jonathan Johnson

Local Wonders: Seasons
in the Bohemian Alps
by Ted Kooser

A Certain Loneliness:
A Memoir
by Sandra Gail Lambert

Bigger than Life:
A Murder, a Memoir
by Dinah Lenney

What Becomes You
by Aaron Raz Link and Hilda Raz

Queen of the Fall: A Memoir
of Girls and Goddesses
by Sonja Livingston

The Virgin of Prince Street:
Expeditions into Devotion
by Sonja Livingston

Such a Life
by Lee Martin

Turning Bones
by Lee Martin

In Rooms of Memory: Essays
by Hilary Masters

Island in the City: A Memoir
by Micah McCrary

Between Panic and Desire
by Dinty W. Moore

Meander Belt: Family, Loss,
and Coming of Age in the
Working-Class South
by M. Randal O'Wain

Sleep in Me
by Jon Pineda

The Solace of Stones: Finding
a Way through Wilderness
by Julie Riddle

Works Cited: An Alphabetical
Odyssey of Mayhem and
Misbehavior
by Brandon R. Schrand

Thoughts from a
Queen-Sized Bed
by Mimi Schwartz

My Ruby Slippers:
The Road Back to Kansas
by Tracy Seeley

To order or obtain more information on these or other University of
Nebraska Press titles, visit nebraskapress.unl.edu.